TO OUR BELOVED FRIEND

BINYAMIN HIRSCH ז״ל

YOUR MEMORY IS
ALWAYS WITH US

WITH LOVE,

FRIENDS EVERYWHERE

In Memory
of
Alfred H. Reznitsky

WHO TO THIS DAY
IS A
BEACON OF LIGHT
FOR HIS WIFE, CHILDREN,
AND GRANDCHILDREN

The Carlebach הגדה של פסח Haggadah

Seder Night
with
Reb Shlomo

Edited by
Chaim Stefansky

URIM PUBLICATIONS
New York • Jerusalem

Urim Publications
POB 52287, 91521 Jerusalem, Israel
Tel: 02-566-0064
E-mail: Publisher@UrimPublications.com

Lambda Publishers, Inc.
3709 13th Ave., Brooklyn, NY 11218 USA
Tel: 718-972-5449, Fax: 718-972-6307
E-mail: mh@ejudaica.com

Website: www.UrimPublications.com

ISBN 965-7108-31-4

Special thanks to Laser Cohen of ELC Music & Computer Services for producing the many Hebrew
graphics used in this Haggadah.

Cover photo: Eli Moshe Klein

Thanks

to
my friend, Betzalel

About This Haggadah

There are so many Haggados already, you're bound to ask why we need another one. The answer is that many people feel a void nowadays where they ought to be tasting the taste of freedom. (After all, that is the feeling we're supposed to enter Pesach with.) We've tried to fill the void with this Haggadah, accompanied with Reb Shlomo Carlebach's Torah. There are thoughts and stories that he told over many years, at many different places, and on many different occasions. It's all told in his own words with scarcely any change.

Where to start? The best place would be with a story Reb Shlomo himself told many times, and which we believe would be his starting point for the Seder.

I was in Waco, Texas, and I was heading for a *mikveh* there. I'm just about to walk in when a big limousine pulls up. Somebody steps out of the car, with a big cowboy hat on his head and chains around his neck — he looks so not Jewish. He starts heading toward the *mikveh*, and I ask him, "Who are you?" He says to me, "I want you to know who I am. You're probably wondering what I'm doing here — obviously, a person who goes to the *mikveh* should also keep Shabbos. Well, I come from a little village near Vizhnitz. From there my family came to America.

"The Shabbos before we left, my father took us to the *heilige* Rebbe Yisrael Vizhnitzer. There were so many hundreds, maybe thousands of Chassidim there, my father told me I might be crushed. So at the end of *davening* my father took me and put me under the table next to the Rebbe — he said that there, at least, I'd be safe. The Rebbe knew I was sitting there, and he gave me challah and fish. He took care of me the whole time.

"Then the Rebbe started saying Torah. I didn't understand it, but suddenly I had a feeling that something special was happening. I saw the Rebbe get up, and he was *mamash* crying. The Rebbe said, 'Yidden, I want you to listen to me. Sometimes a *Yid* wants to do a mitzvah and then Brother Devil comes along and says, "What are you, crazy? Now you're doing mitzvos, but I know what you did wrong before and I know your plans for later. Who are you fooling now when you do a mitzvah?"'

"The Rebbe began yelling, 'Yidden, tell the Devil in my name, "Please leave me alone for one minute. I don't care what I'll do later; right now I want to serve God."' He sat down, put his holy hand under the table and laid it on my head. He said to me, 'Do you hear what I'm saying? I beg you never to forget.'"

The stranger says to me, "I want you to know, I'm here in Texas; I don't usually keep Shabbos. I usually eat on Yom Kippur, but sometimes I fast. I hate to say bad things, but the Evil Inclination is my master. But from time to time I *mamash* want to do something holy. This afternoon, I don't know why, I had a feeling I've got to go to the *mikveh*. A little voice tells me, 'You're crazy. You don't keep Shabbos. What are you going to the *mikveh* for?' But I'm going, for this one minute."

On Pesach, the Seder night, we're crying and begging, "Give us these few minutes to feel as if we're leaving Egypt right now." We're leaving the *galus* that we sit in all year round. We wear a white *kittel* to become like the holy angels. We want to be beyond ourselves, beyond the exterior, shallow things. We want to be heavenly, beyond time. Let's take these few infinite moments of freedom with us throughout our lives.

סדר

ערב פסח

Preparing

for

the Seder

בדיקת חמץ

The search for *chametz* begins upon nightfall of the fourteenth day of Nisan. We must search all areas where *chametz* may have been brought during the course of the year, even if a thorough cleaning was done before Passover. The search should not be interrupted until its completion (except for an interruption relating to the search). If the Seder falls on Saturday night the search is made on Thursday night. There is a custom to distribute ten pieces of *chametz* through the house before the search. Care should be taken to list the locations of these pieces.
Before the search for *chametz* begins the following blessing is recited:

בָּרוּךְ אַתָּה יְיָ אֱלֹהֵינוּ מֶלֶךְ הָעוֹלָם אֲשֶׁר קִדְּשָׁנוּ בְּמִצְוֹתָיו וְצִוָּנוּ עַל בִּעוּר חָמֵץ:

After the search one should wrap the *chametz* and put it in a safe place. Then the following declaration is made. The declaration must be understood in order to take effect. Any *chametz* that you still want to use is not included in the declaration.

כָּל חֲמִירָא וַחֲמִיעָא דְּאִכָּא בִּרְשׁוּתִי, דְּלָא חֲמִתֵּהּ וּדְלָא בַעַרְתֵּהּ וּדְלָא יְדַעְנָא לֵיהּ, לִבְטִיל וְלֶהֱוֵי הֶפְקֵר כְּעַפְרָא דְאַרְעָא.

ביעור חמץ

On the morning after the search, before ten o'clock, we burn all existing *chametz* and the following declaration is made. Its meaning must be understood. If the seder falls on Saturday night, this declaration is made on Shabbos morning; however, the burning takes place on Friday morning. Any *chametz* remaining from the Shabbos morning meal is flushed down the toilet. After burning or, on Shabbos, flushing, the declaration is made.

כָּל חֲמִירָא וַחֲמִיעָא דְּאִכָּא בִּרְשׁוּתִי, דַּחֲזִיתֵהּ וּדְלָא חֲזִיתֵהּ, דַּחֲמִיתֵהּ וּדְלָא חֲמִתֵּהּ, דְּבִעַרְתֵּהּ וּדְלָא בִעַרְתֵּהּ, לִבָּטֵל וְלֶהֱוֵי הֶפְקֵר כְּעַפְרָא דְאַרְעָא.

בדיקת חמץ   **The Search for Chametz**

We came out of Egypt in the month of Nisan, in the spring. Everything

The Search for Chametz

The search for *chametz* begins upon nightfall of the fourteenth day of Nissan. We must search all areas where *chametz* may have been brought during the course of the year, even if a thorough cleaning was done before Passover. The search should not be interrupted until its completion (except for an interruption relating to the search). If the Seder falls on Saturday night the search is made on Thursday night. There is a custom to distribute ten pieces of *chametz* through the house before the search. Care should be taken to list the locations of these pieces.

Before the search for *chametz* begins the following blessing is recited:

Blessed are You, Hashem, our God, King of the universe, Who has sanctified us with His commandments and has commanded us to remove all chametz from our possession.

After the search one should wrap the *chametz* and put it in a safe place. Then the following declaration is made. The declaration must be understood in order to take effect. Any *chametz* that you still want to use is not included in the declaration.

All leaven that is in my possession which I have not seen, have not removed and do not know about, should be as if it does not exist and should become ownerless, like the dust of the earth.

Burning the Chametz

On the morning after the search, before ten o'clock, we burn all existing *chametz* and the following declaration is made. Its meaning must be understood. If the seder falls on Saturday night, this declaration is made on Shabbos morning; however, the burning takes place on Friday morning. Any *chametz* remaining from the Shabbos morning meal is flushed down the toilet. After burning or, on Shabbos, flushing, the declaration is made.

All leaven that is in my possession, whether I have seen it or not, which I have removed or not, should be as if it does not exist and should become owner-less, like the dust of the earth.

is becoming free, every flower, every blade of grass; colors are returning to

עֵירוּב תַּבְשִׁילִין

When Passover falls on Thursday, an *eiruv tavshilin* must be made on Wednesday for it to be permissible to cook on Yom Tov for Shabbos. The *eiruv* indicates that preparations for Shabbos have begun before Yom Tov. The head of the household takes some matzah and any cooked food and sets them aside until Shabbos, to be used on Shabbos. He then recites the following:

בָּרוּךְ אַתָּה יְיָ אֱלֹהֵינוּ מֶלֶךְ הָעוֹלָם אֲשֶׁר קִדְּשָׁנוּ בְּמִצְוֹתָיו
וְצִוָּנוּ עַל מִצְוַת עֵרוּב.

בַּהֲדֵין עֵרוּבָא יְהֵא שָׁרֵי לָנָא לְמֵיפָא וּלְבַשָּׁלָא וּלְאַטְמָנָא
וּלְאַדְלָקָא שְׁרָגָא, וּלְמֶעְבַּד כָּל צָרְכָנָא, מִיּוֹמָא טָבָא
לְשַׁבַּתָּא, לָנוּ וּלְכָל יִשְׂרָאֵל הַדָּרִים בָּעִיר הַזֹּאת.

the world as the leaves and the flowers come out from hiding, reminding us that they can't be suppressed forever. There's so much freedom in the air, so much sweetness. What keeps us from being free sometimes is a very small thing. *Chametz* is *assur b'mashehu* — it's forbidden for us to have even the smallest amount of it in our possession, because sometimes one crumb can destroy your life.

You know, friends, most married couples that get divorced do it not because of a major event, but because of small events — tiny crumbs. As Pesach comes we're getting rid of all those tiny crumbs. Between redemption and slavery is a *mashehu*, a crumb, a speck. Between being a good father, a good mother, and not being proper parents is just a *mashehu*, something so tiny. Real redemption comes when we walk around with a candle and find this tiny trait that's holding us back from being what we could be, this little thing that's in essence ruining us — when we find it and burn it.

בִּעוּר חָמֵץ   **Burning the Chametz**

The Karliner says, "How do you burn the *chametz?* With the fire of your heart, with the fire of serving God." And the fire goes on burning all through

Eiruv Tavshilin

When Passover falls on Thursday, an *eiruv tavshilin* must be made on Wednesday for it to be permissible to cook on Yom Tov for Shabbos. The *eiruv* indicates that preparations for Shabbos have begun before Yom Tov. The head of the household takes some matzah and any cooked food and sets them aside until Shabbos, to be used on Shabbos. He then recites the following:

Blessed are You, Hashem, our God, King of the universe, Who has sanctified us with His commandments and has commanded us to observe the mitzvah of eiruv.

By means of this eiruv it shall be permitted to bake, cook, keep food warm, kindle flame and make all necessary preparations on Yom Tov for the Shabbos (for ourselves and for all Jews who live in this city).

Pesach. The *heilige* Rebbe David Lelover says, "I once learned how to serve God from the Cossacks. I was passing by a fort where Cossacks got their basic training, and I saw them beating another Cossack as a punishment. I asked them, 'What did he do?' and they answered, 'Last night he was standing guard, and in the morning we found him half frozen.' I said he should be given a medal, since despite the cold he held out. The Cossacks laughed and said, 'You don't understand! If you're really serving the Czar of Russia, everything you do gets done with so much fire, it keeps you warm.'" So on Pesach we are really serving God, once we found the *chametz* and burned it and our hearts are on fire.

הַדְלָקַת נֵרוֹת

The blessing is recited and then the candles are lit.

בָּרוּךְ אַתָּה יְהֹוָה אֱלֹהֵינוּ מֶלֶךְ הָעוֹלָם אֲשֶׁר קִדְּשָׁנוּ
בְּמִצְוֹתָיו וְצִוָּנוּ לְהַדְלִיק נֵר שֶׁל יוֹם טוֹב.

When Yom Tov falls on Shabbos, first we light the candles, then recite the following blessing:

בָּרוּךְ אַתָּה יְהֹוָה אֱלֹהֵינוּ מֶלֶךְ הָעוֹלָם אֲשֶׁר קִדְּשָׁנוּ
בְּמִצְוֹתָיו וְצִוָּנוּ לְהַדְלִיק נֵר שֶׁל שַׁבָּת וְשֶׁל יוֹם טוֹב.

It is better for women not to say *Shehecheyanu* when they light the Yom Tov candles. The best thing is for them to say Amen to their husband's *berachah* when he says Kiddush. If a woman did say *Shehecheyanu* at candle-lighting, then it is best for her not to answer Amen to her husband's *Shehecheyanu* later on (although some *poskim* say it is permitted).

בָּרוּךְ אַתָּה יְהֹוָה אֱלֹהֵינוּ מֶלֶךְ הָעוֹלָם שֶׁהֶחֱיָנוּ וְקִיְּמָנוּ
וְהִגִּיעָנוּ לַזְּמַן הַזֶּה.

הדלקת נרות   **Candle-Lighting**

The Viletniker Rebbe told this story about his mother: "When my mother lit the holy lights for Shabbos and Yom Tov, you couldn't imagine a Cohen in the *Beis Hamikdash*, the Holy Temple, crying for Israel with more tears than she shed for my brother and me. One Friday night she lit the candles, and the time went by and it was already Shabbos, and she was still praying over her lights. Her tears poured down over them and actually put them out. When she opened her eyes she saw the room was dark. She said, '*Ribbono shel Olam*, our dear Father, don't you know the truth, that I can't live without my Shabbos candles? Master of the world, You come and light my *Shabbosdike licht* again.' And I swear to you," said the Rebbe, "I saw a hand come from Heaven and relight my mother's Shabbos candles."

You know, my sweet friends, this story is deep in my heart, and I'm sure in yours, too. We're living in an age in the world when we've seen so many candles blown out. We saw six million of them blown out — so many *Yidden* all over the world whose light isn't shining anymore. So I'm crying and

Candle-Lighting

The blessing is recited and then the candles are lit. When Yom Tov falls on Shabbos, first we light the candles, then we recite the blessing with the words in the parentheses added.

Blessed are you, Hashem, our God, King of the universe, Who has sanctified us with His commandments and has commanded us to kindle the light (of the Shabbos and) of Yom Tov.

It is better for women not to say Shehecheyanu when they light the Yom Tov candles. The best thing is for them to say Amen to their husband's berachah when he says Kiddush. If a woman did say Shehecheyanu at candle-lighting, then it is best for her not to answer Amen to her husband's Shehecheyanu later on (although some poskim say it is permitted).

Blessed are you, Hashem, our God, King of the universe, Who has kept us alive, sustained us, and enabled us to reach this season.

begging, in your name and in my name: let there be a hand from Heaven to relight our Bobbe's *Shabbosdike licht*. Let the Shabbos lights that are burning now keep burning until the great morning comes. Please don't blow out any more lights; this is the prayer of every Jewish parent when we light the holy lights.

קערת הסדר

The Seder should not begin before nightfall. Matzah, bitter herbs, a shank bone, an egg, and charoses (compounded of fruit, nuts and wine) are placed in one of the three arrangements shown below, according to the custom of the house.

According to the Rama

According to the Vilna Gaon

According to the Ari ז"ל
(the matzos are placed under the plate,
usually on shelves)

The Seder Plate

The Seder should not begin before nightfall. Matzah, bitter herbs, a shank bone, an egg, and charoses (compounded of fruit, nuts and wine) are placed in one of the three arrangements shown below, according to the custom of the house.

According to the Rama

According to the Vilna Gaon

According to the Ari ז"ל
(the matzos are placed under the plate, usually on shelves)

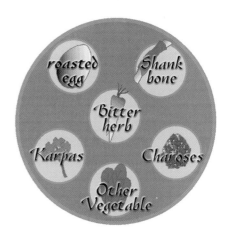

סדר

ליל פסח

The

Seder

Night

סִימָנֵי הַסֵּדֶר

כּוֹרֵךְ מָרוֹר	קַדֵּשׁ וּרְחַץ
עוֹרֵךְ שֻׁלְחָן	כַּרְפַּס יַחַץ
בָּרֵךְ צָפוּן	מַגִּיד רָחְצָה
נִרְצָה הַלֵּל	מוֹצִיא מַצָּה

The Order of the Seder   סימני הסדר

I remember it — when we were little, my brother and sister and I would sit down at the table on Seder night. My father would begin telling us, "Children, tonight we all are kings, we all are princes. We are eating at God's table." I can remember how our eyes were glowing.

The beginning is when we call out "*Kaddesh*, make me holy! Master of the world, all year long I thought so little of myself. I didn't know how holy I could be. Tonight I know I could be so holy; I'm begging you, *kaddesh*, make me so holy. Make my children so holy, make the world so holy."

Then we say *Ur'chatz*. All year long, when I see someone with a dirty face, or a little dust on their *neshamah*, on their soul, I turn away. This night I say, "Master of the world, I would love to be a cleaning man tonight. I have a little soap — I have matzah, and it's the holiest soap in the world. Matzah is just flour and water; no air, nothing blown out of proportion, it's the real thing. One piece of matzah cleanses the soul. Please let me clean the world."

The Order of the Seder

Many people have the custom to announce the name of each section at its appropriate time throughout the Seder.

Kaddesh	Recitation of Kiddush
Ur'chatz	Wash the hands before eating karpas
Karpas	Eat a vegetable dipped in salt water
Yachatz	Break the middle matzah, and hide the larger half for the Afikoman
Maggid	Recite the story of Passover
Rochtzah	Wash the hands before the meal
Motzi	Say the Hamotzi blessing
Matzah	Eat the matzah
Maror	Eat the bitter herbs
Korech	Eat matzah and bitter herbs together
Shulchan Orech	Eat the Yom Tov meal
Tzafun	Eat the Afikoman
Barech	Say Grace After Meals
Hallel	Sing the Hallel Psalms
Nirtzah	Conclude the Seder and pray that God accept it and speedily send the Mashiach

The Koznitzer Maggid says about *Yachatz*, "The world is so broken, but our children can make the world whole again. We break the matzah; the small piece we keep, and the big piece — the bigger brokenness — our children take away. Then they bring it back to us whole, to serve as the *Afikoman* at the end of the seder." Our children: they are the ones that are

קַדֵּשׁ

The matzos are covered. Everyone at the table should have a glass of wine that holds the proper quantity necessary to fulfill the mitzvah of the Four Cups. On Shabbos night begin here:

וַיְהִי עֶרֶב וַיְהִי בֹקֶר

יוֹם הַשִּׁשִּׁי וַיְכֻלּוּ הַשָּׁמַיִם וְהָאָרֶץ וְכָל צְבָאָם: וַיְכַל אֱלֹהִים בַּיּוֹם הַשְּׁבִיעִי מְלַאכְתּוֹ אֲשֶׁר עָשָׂה וַיִּשְׁבֹּת בַּיּוֹם הַשְּׁבִיעִי מִכָּל מְלַאכְתּוֹ אֲשֶׁר עָשָׂה: וַיְבָרֶךְ אֱלֹהִים אֶת יוֹם הַשְּׁבִיעִי וַיְקַדֵּשׁ אֹתוֹ כִּי בוֹ שָׁבַת מִכָּל מְלַאכְתּוֹ אֲשֶׁר בָּרָא אֱלֹהִים לַעֲשׂוֹת:

taking brokenness away from us.

You know, friends, sometimes I come home from a concert at four o'clock in the morning, and I'm dead tired. After that, if anybody woke me up at five o'clock I would be angry. But if my children wake me up, oh, it's so beautiful! Master of the world, how can I thank you for children? They're so perfect, so good. I don't want them to grow up in a broken world.

Broken doesn't mean that you're broken by pain and sadness. Broken means that we don't know what's good and what's evil, we don't know whether we know or we don't know. Master of the world, redeem us!

קַדֵּשׁ   **Kaddesh**

All year long, wine may make us drunk; but Seder night we're drunk with freedom. We know that You have chosen us to show the world what freedom is. Freedom doesn't mean I can do what I want. It means I'm free to serve God, to correct my *neshamah*, to perfect the world.

Kaddesh

The matzos are covered. Everyone at the table should have a glass of wine that holds the proper quantity necessary to fulfill the mitzvah of the Four Cups. On Shabbos night begin here:

(It was evening and it was morning,) the sixth day. The heaven and the earth and all their array were finished. God completed on the seventh day His work which He had done, and He rested on the seventh day from all His work which He had done. God blessed the seventh day and made it holy, because on it He rested from all His work which God created.

Wine... the grape has to go through so much pain until it becomes wine. When it's wine at last, it's so beautiful. We have to go through so much until we reach where we have to be. You know, if you asked the grape about it in the middle of the process, the grape would say, "Do you know what I'm going through? Everybody steps on me. Once I was so beautiful — look what has happened to me now!" But I would tell the grape, "Wait; soon, soon...."

The Izhbitzer Rebbe says that wine is the symbol of the forces in the world which make us forget what we really are, the ones which dehumanize us. An alcoholic is capable of destroying himself, as well as his family and friends. You know what I do? I take the cup of wine in my hand and I say, "There's no power in the world that can make me forget there is only one God."

In this world, when you want to show you're the master, you put yourself above the others by putting them down. But with God, how does He show He's the master? He says, "I lift the others up." You remember, when we were Pharaoh's slaves in Egypt, we were downhearted. We were broken. Then we became servants of God. You know what God did to us? He lifted us up! So, according to our holy tradition, we lift up the cup of wine. You lift it up to the same level your heart is at.

On all other nights begin here. On Shabbos night include all words in parentheses:

בָּרוּךְ אַתָּה יְיָ אֱלֹהֵינוּ מֶלֶךְ הָעוֹלָם בּוֹרֵא פְּרִי הַגָּפֶן
בָּרוּךְ אַתָּה יְיָ אֱלֹהֵינוּ מֶלֶךְ הָעוֹלָם אֲשֶׁר בָּחַר בָּנוּ מִכָּל עָם
וְרוֹמְמָנוּ מִכָּל לָשׁוֹן וְקִדְּשָׁנוּ בְּמִצְוֹתָיו וַתִּתֶּן לָנוּ יְיָ אֱלֹהֵינוּ
בְּאַהֲבָה (לשבת: שַׁבָּתוֹת לִמְנוּחָה וּ) מוֹעֲדִים לְשִׂמְחָה
חַגִּים וּזְמַנִּים לְשָׂשׂוֹן אֶת יוֹם (לשבת:הַשַּׁבָּת הַזֶּה וְאֶת יוֹם)
חַג הַמַּצּוֹת הַזֶּה זְמַן חֵרוּתֵנוּ (לשבת:בְּאַהֲבָה) מִקְרָא קֹדֶשׁ
זֵכֶר לִיצִיאַת מִצְרָיִם כִּי בָנוּ בָחַרְתָּ וְאוֹתָנוּ קִדַּשְׁתָּ מִכָּל
הָעַמִּים (לשבת:וְשַׁבָּת) וּמוֹעֲדֵי קָדְשֶׁךָ (לשבת:בְּאַהֲבָה)
וּבְרָצוֹן בְּשִׂמְחָה וּבְשָׂשׂוֹן הִנְחַלְתָּנוּ. בָּרוּךְ אַתָּה יְיָ מְקַדֵּשׁ
(לשבת:הַשַּׁבָּת) וְיִשְׂרָאֵל וְהַזְּמַנִּים:

וקדשנו במצותיו **Who made us holy with His mitzvos**

I want to tell you about a holy Jew, how he fulfilled and sanctified himself through the mitzvah of *tzedakah,* the most God-like act in the world. When a person has the privilege to give, he is so close to Hashem.

It was the year 1550, and we were so persecuted and poor. In the ghetto of Cracow there was one rich Jew whose name was Yossele. He was rich, but he was also the greatest miser in the world. In his whole life nobody had ever seen him give a penny to a single Jew. "He must have a heart of stone," they all thought. — You know, my friends, a miser isn't part of the world, because the world was created by God just so He could have someone to give to. The whole world is here for the sake of giving, and if you don't give as Hashem does, you're not part of His world. — Nobody said "Gut Shabbos" to Yossele; no one gave him a blessing on Rosh Hashanah. When Yossele walked in the street, people would call at him, "Dirty miser."

One day the Burial Society were told that Yossele was dying. They rushed to his bedside and said, "All right, here's your last chance. You never gave anything to the poor. Make up for it now! Give us a thousand rubles to pay for your grave. We'll give every penny of it to the poor." But obviously Yossele really did have a heart of stone. He answered them, "I can't afford more than fifty rubles." They got so angry, they started yelling, "Yossele, you

On all other nights begin here. On Shabbos night include all words in parentheses:

Blessed are You, Hashem, our God, King of the universe, Creator of the fruit of the vine.

Blessed are You, Hashem, our God, King of the universe, Who has chosen us from all nations and exalted us above all tongues, and sanctified us with His commandments. You have given us, Hashem our God, with love (Shabbos for rest and) festivals for happiness, festivals and seasons for joy: (this Shabbos and this) Festival of Matzos, season of our freedom (in love), a holy convocation in remembrance of the Exodus from Egypt. For You have chosen us and sanctified us above all nations, and You gave us (the Shabbos and) Your holy festivals (with love and with favor), with gladness and joy, as a heritage. Blessed are You, Hashem, Who sanctifies (the Sabbath and) Israel, and the festive seasons.

know you can't take your money with you!" He just said, "No, I'm not giving more than fifty."

In the end they gave up and said, "Fine, but we're not going to bury you." Yossele just smiled and said, "Then I'll bury myself. I've done a lot by myself, you know." The Burial Society didn't know what he meant. They shook their heads and got up to walk out, and at that moment he said *"Shema Yisrael Hashem Elokeinu Hashem Echad"* and passed away. Well, they kept their word. Yossele died on Sunday night, and they left his body there in the house. They didn't bury him on Monday, not on Tuesday or on Wednesday. Wednesday night one of his neighbors decided that he couldn't just leave him lying there, so he threw Yossele on a wagon and drove out to the cemetery. Still, Yossele had been a miser: so he buried him outside of the cemetery, under a tree.

If Yom Tov falls on Saturday night, the following is recited:

בָּרוּךְ אַתָּה יְיָ אֱלֹהֵינוּ מֶלֶךְ הָעוֹלָם בּוֹרֵא מְאוֹרֵי הָאֵשׁ:

בָּרוּךְ אַתָּה יְיָ אֱלֹהֵינוּ מֶלֶךְ הָעוֹלָם הַמַּבְדִּיל בֵּין קֹדֶשׁ לְחֹל

בֵּין אוֹר לְחֹשֶׁךְ בֵּין יִשְׂרָאֵל לָעַמִּים בֵּין יוֹם הַשְּׁבִיעִי לְשֵׁשֶׁת

יְמֵי הַמַּעֲשֶׂה. בֵּין קְדֻשַּׁת שַׁבָּת לִקְדֻשַּׁת יוֹם טוֹב הִבְדַּלְתָּ

וְאֶת יוֹם הַשְּׁבִיעִי מִשֵּׁשֶׁת יְמֵי הַמַּעֲשֶׂה קִדַּשְׁתָּ. הִבְדַּלְתָּ

וְקִדַּשְׁתָּ אֶת עַמְּךָ יִשְׂרָאֵל בִּקְדֻשָּׁתֶךָ. בָּרוּךְ אַתָּה יְיָ

הַמַּבְדִּיל בֵּין קֹדֶשׁ לְקֹדֶשׁ:

On all nights conclude here:

בָּרוּךְ אַתָּה יְיָ אֱלֹהֵינוּ מֶלֶךְ הָעוֹלָם שֶׁהֶחֱיָנוּ וְקִיְּמָנוּ וְהִגִּיעָנוּ

לַזְּמַן הַזֶּה:

The wine should be drunk without delay while reclining on the left side.

Open your hearts, dear friends. This was not the end of the story. The Chief Rabbi of Cracow in those days was R. Kalman, who was a great scholar. Late Thursday night a poor man knocked on the Rav's door and said, "Rebbe, I need some money to buy food for the holy Shabbos." R. Kalman said to him, "I'll be happy to give you money, but tell me: I've known you for such a long time, and you never asked for *tzedakah* before. Why are you asking me today for the first time?" The poor man said, "Rebbe, I want you to know that for twenty years I haven't been able to make a living. But every Thursday morning, all these years, I've found an envelope under my door, and on it was written '*lekhovod Shabbos,* in honor of Shabbos.' Today, though, there was no letter."

R. Kalman gave his poor neighbor enough to make Shabbos with, and went back to learning. Two minutes later there was another knock at the door. It was another poor man asking for money for Shabbos. The Rav asked him the same question, "Why didn't you come and ask last week or the week before?" The man said, "For the last ten years, I've found an envelope containing two rubles under my door every Thursday morning." Well, all that night poor people came knocking at the Rav's door, and each one told about an envelope that used to appear under his door. One had five rubles in it, another had two, and in yet another was ten rubles, all *lekhovod Shabbos.*

If Yom Tov falls on Saturday night, the following is recited:

Blessed are You, Hashem, our God, King of the universe, Creator of lights of fire.

Blessed are You, Hashem, our God, King of the universe, Who distinguishes between holiness and secular, between light and darkness, between Israel and nations, between the seventh day and the six days of activity. You have made a distinction between the holiness of Shabbos and the holiness of Yom Tov; and You have sanctified the seventh day above the six days of labor. You distinguished and sanctified Your nation, Israel, with Your holiness. Blessed are You, Hashem, who distinguishes between holiness (of Shabbos) and holiness (of Yom Tov).

On all nights conclude here:

Blessed are You, Hashem, our God, King of the universe, Who has kept us alive, sustained us, and enabled us to reach this season.

The wine should be drunk without delay while reclining on the left side.

R. Kalman asked a lot of questions the next day, and in the end he discovered that all this had been the work of Yossele the Miser. He was so heartbroken! They hadn't even buried him. He also wondered something; he asked the poor people, "How did Yossele know you so well? How did he know how much to give each one of you?" This is what they said: "Every one of us thought at one point in his life that maybe he could get through to Yossele. We knocked at his door, and he invited us in with so much love and sweetness that we opened our hearts to him. Yossele would sit us down

וּרְחַץ

The hands are washed without a blessing.

כַּרְפַּס

Everyone at the Seder takes a piece of a vegetable, dips it into salt water, and recites the following blessing. You should have in mind that this blessing includes the *maror* which is eaten later on in the Seder.

בָּרוּךְ אַתָּה יְיָ אֱלֹהֵינוּ מֶלֶךְ הָעוֹלָם בּוֹרֵא פְּרִי הָאֲדָמָה:

יַחַץ

The leader of the Seder breaks the middle matzah in half. He keeps the smaller part and wraps up the larger part for later use as the *Afikoman*. The Seder plate is removed.

and say, 'Sweetest friend, tell me everything.' He'd take out paper and pen and write down all the details: name, address, how many in the family — everything. He'd say, 'My heart is bleeding, you must be starving! How much do you need each week in order to live?' We'd say, 'Yossele, if only you could give me five rubles a week, to keep my children alive." Just then Yossele would get up and bring in some food, and he'd talk about everything in the world except *tzedakah*. Then all of a sudden he'd jump up like a crazy man and throw us out, yelling 'Do you really think I'm crazy enough to give you my precious money? Go away and never come back!'" The poor people would go home and tell their wives that Yossele was crazy. And Thursday morning there was an envelope under the door.

R. Kalman was beside himself. Yossele, who had kept all the poor people in the city alive and never wanted any *kovod* for it — they hadn't even buried him! And the same children he had kept alive had mocked him all the time. Now what?

That Shabbos he announced in the *shul* that Sunday would be a fast day, to beg forgiveness from Yossele the Holy Miser. The whole community came to *shul* that day and they cried endlessly, "Yossele, forgive us." Just at sunset Rav Kalman went up to the Holy Ark, opened it, and yelled out from the

Ur'chatz

The hands are washed without a blessing.

Karpas

Everyone at the Seder takes a piece of a vegetable, dips it into salt water, and recites the following blessing. You should have in mind that this blessing includes the *maror* which is eaten later on in the Seder.

Blessed are You, Hashem, our God, King of the universe, Creator of the fruits of the earth.

Yachatz

The leader of the Seder breaks the middle matzah in half. He keeps the smaller part and wraps up the larger part for later use as the *Afikoman*. The Seder plate is removed.

deepest depths of his heart, "Yossele, Holy Miser, give us a sign that you forgive us!" and he fainted. When he woke up he told the people what he saw when he was unconscious:

"In my dream I saw Yossele sitting up in Heaven, shining. He said, 'Please tell all my brothers and sisters to go home and not to worry. There's no need to ask me for forgiveness — don't you understand, this is the way I wanted it to be. I wanted the privilege of giving *tzedakah* without anybody knowing; only the One who knows everything needed to know. I also wanted to be sure that nobody would ever thank me or reward me except Him. So please thank all the poor people who came to my house, and tell them that because of them I'm sitting here next to our father Avraham and our mother Sarah. I have everything now that I ever wanted — except for one thing. I'd give up all of Paradise for just one more Thursday morning. Rebbe, there are no poor people in heaven, no doors waiting for *tzedakah,* no envelopes to put under them!'

"I was still worried about one thing, and I asked him, 'But how did it feel to be buried alone?' Yossele answered, 'I wasn't alone. Avraham, Yitzchak, and Yaakov, our four mothers, Moshe, Aaron, Yosef and David were all there. King David walked behind me playing a song, and Eliyahu Hanavi walked in front of me holding a candle.'"

מגיד

The Story

of

the Exodus

מַגִּיד

The leader of the Seder lifts the broken matzah and starts the story of Passover with this short invitation:

הָא לַחְמָא עַנְיָא דִּי אֲכָלוּ אַבְהָתָנָא בְּאַרְעָא דְמִצְרָיִם. כָּל דִּכְפִין יֵיתֵי וְיֵכֻל כָּל־דִּצְרִיךְ יֵיתֵי וְיִפְסַח. הָשַׁתָּא הָכָא. לְשָׁנָה הַבָּאָה בְּאַרְעָא דְיִשְׂרָאֵל. הָשַׁתָּא עַבְדֵי. לְשָׁנָה הַבָּאָה בְּנֵי חוֹרִין:

Whoever is hungry   כל דכפין

"*Kol dichfin, yeisei v'yeichul*, whoever is hungry, let him come and eat." Friends, this is our generation. This is you and I, but most of all it's our children. There's such a hunger in the world for something beautiful, something holy — a hunger for one good word, one holy word, one message from God. People are hungry for something lofty, glorious. So this is my wish for all of us: let the hungry people get together, everyone who's hungry for holiness, for friendship, for love — the people who are hungry to give their children one word from God. Let's get together! Let's you and I fix the world.

Friends, hungry people feel so close to each other. Who's bringing peace to the world? Not the politicians! Not the great orators! Not the great businessmen! Only little hungry people.

I've walked the streets of the world. I've walked in Yerushalayim, in Berlin, in Washington, in Moscow; I've walked in Sydney and in Copenhagen. The world is hungry, so hungry. Sometimes people stop you on the street and ask you, "What time is it?" They have a watch. Do you know what they're telling you? "Half of my life is gone and I'm still hungry. Maybe you have a good word for me?"

Some people ask you, "Where's the next street?" They're not idiots. They could find it if they wanted. They're telling you, "I don't know where to go. — I have the address. — I'm a rich man; I have everything; but I don't know where I'm going. Maybe you have a message from God, from someone that loves me — a message to show me the way to fill my heart, to fill my soul?"

"*Hashata hacha*, this year we are here, next year may we be in the land of Israel." Yerushalayim, the holy city, is the headquarters of the hungry people. Someday the hungry people will get together.

Maggid

The leader of the Seder lifts the broken matzah and starts the story of Passover with this short invitation:

This is the bread of affliction which our fathers ate in the land of Egypt. Whoever is hungry, let him come and eat. Whoever is needy, let him come and celebrate Pesach! Now we are here; next year may we be in the Land of Israel! Now we are slaves; next year may we be free men!

This is my prayer for your children and my children: let's all get together, the whole world, wherever you are! Let's all get together, pray together, pour out our hearts together.

At the same time, remember all the good people of the world who were here before us. They prayed for us, and they pray with us now. Let the day be soon when the whole world gets together in Yerushalayim, the Holy City. This is what the Prophet says: "*Ki beisi beis tefillah l'chol ha'amim,* My house is the house of prayer for all nations."

Do you know what we're saying? "All who are hungry, come and eat." Is there anybody in the world who needs food? Is there anybody in the world who is broken and needs a friend? Tonight is the night! My door is open, my heart is open. It's open because all the gates of Heaven are open. On Seder night I'm so real, I'm so close. Heaven and Earth are close to each other.

What was the first great thing Avraham did after he became a Jew? The Torah tells us: the first thing he did was to welcome strangers into his home.

Whatever you do that's between you and other people, that's what you're doing between you and God. Until Avraham, God was a stranger in the world. Avraham's whole mission was to bring God into the world. And see, what Avraham did between him and God is the same as what he did between him and people. He brought God into the world; he brought strangers into his home. Avraham's welcoming in strangers brought God's light in to

The matzos are uncovered and the Haggadah is said in unison.

מַה נִּשְׁתַּנָּה הַלַּיְלָה הַזֶּה מִכָּל הַלֵּילוֹת: שֶׁבְּכָל הַלֵּילוֹת אָנוּ
אוֹכְלִין חָמֵץ וּמַצָּה. הַלַּיְלָה הַזֶּה כֻּלּוֹ מַצָּה: שֶׁבְּכָל הַלֵּילוֹת
אָנוּ אוֹכְלִין שְׁאָר יְרָקוֹת. הַלַּיְלָה הַזֶּה מָרוֹר: שֶׁבְּכָל הַלֵּילוֹת
אֵין אָנוּ מַטְבִּילִין אֲפִלּוּ פַּעַם אֶחָת. הַלַּיְלָה הַזֶּה שְׁתֵּי
פְעָמִים: שֶׁבְּכָל הַלֵּילוֹת אָנוּ אוֹכְלִין בֵּין יוֹשְׁבִין וּבֵין מְסֻבִּין.
הַלַּיְלָה הַזֶּה כֻּלָּנוּ מְסֻבִּין:

places where nothing else could reach to bring it in. To welcome a stranger means that I take you into my house: and my house should be so beautiful, so full of holiness, that by bringing you into it I put you up on a higher level than where you were before. Even just for those few minutes that you are in my house, you are high up.

Children are the greatest strangers in the world. While Avraham was welcoming angels, he was learning how to welcome Yitzchak. The saddest thing in the world is to be away from your children, when your children are strangers to you. When we, God's children, are so far away from Him, it's so sad.

A slave is someone who is not free to be himself. He thinks, "I do everything right but I'm alienated from each thing that I do, because I'm not doing it freely, because I choose to, because I want to — only because I have to do it. But if I can be a free person, then all I do is close to me, because now it's really me doing it." On Seder night we're free. We're God's children. We're really serving Him, in the true sense of the word. According to our great Kabbalists, on Seder night, when I'm sitting with my children and they feel so close to me, this is the time I can ask God for anything. Because aren't we God's children?

מה נשתנה   **How is this night different?**

The smallest child begins and then the older children follow. All the children are asking questions. Then, when they're done, we open up our hearts as they did and we ask our children questions in return. Let me ask

The matzos are uncovered and the Haggadah is said in unison.

Why is this night different from all other nights?
On all other nights we eat chametz and matzah, but on this night only matzah.
On all other nights we eat any vegetables, but on this night we eat maror.
On all other nights we do not dip even once, but on this night we dip twice.
On all other nights we eat sitting or reclining, but on this night we all recline.

You four questions, God.

"God in heaven, why is this night so long? Why is exile so long? Above all, I don't understand, how are we so free? We were celebrating Pesach in Auschwitz and in Mauthausen. *Yidden* would get together late at night and they would sing the *Mah Nishtanah*. Master of the world, how come we're so free?" Maybe my feet are in exile, and my hands; but my soul, my inside, my ideas, my culture, my understanding of the world — they're not in exile.

Nowadays we're so in exile, living within Western culture; we're in exile in the perverted thinking of the world. On Seder night you go out from exile; and I hear my children, who are the deepest in the world, the finest, the purest. They say, "Master of the world, tonight everything is matzah. Nothing is blown up, nothing is out of proportion; it's just the way it really is." Because you know what evil does: it blows everything up out of proportion. For example, someone says to me, "How are you?" and I think I don't like the sound, the tone he says it in. I'm already thinking to myself, "I know he wants to insult me." This can start a war. On Seder night everything is so clear. It's so beautiful.

It was 1943, the second night of Pesach: the last seder in the Warsaw ghetto. There was just one bunker left; there was just one Jewish family left, with one Jewish child. Until Mashiach comes there won't be such another Seder.

עֲבָדִים הָיִינוּ לְפַרְעֹה בְּמִצְרָיִם. וַיּוֹצִיאֵנוּ יְיָ אֱלֹהֵינוּ מִשָּׁם בְּיָד
חֲזָקָה וּבִזְרוֹעַ נְטוּיָה. וְאִלּוּ לֹא הוֹצִיא הַקָּדוֹשׁ בָּרוּךְ הוּא
אֶת אֲבוֹתֵינוּ מִמִּצְרַיִם הֲרֵי אָנוּ וּבָנֵינוּ וּבְנֵי בָנֵינוּ מְשֻׁעְבָּדִים
הָיִינוּ לְפַרְעֹה בְּמִצְרָיִם. וַאֲפִלּוּ כֻּלָּנוּ חֲכָמִים כֻּלָּנוּ נְבוֹנִים כֻּלָּנוּ
זְקֵנִים כֻּלָּנוּ יוֹדְעִים אֶת הַתּוֹרָה. מִצְוָה עָלֵינוּ לְסַפֵּר בִּיצִיאַת
מִצְרָיִם. וְכָל הַמַּרְבֶּה לְסַפֵּר בִּיצִיאַת מִצְרַיִם הֲרֵי זֶה מְשֻׁבָּח:

Moishele is asking the *Mah Nishtanah*: "Why do we go through such pain, more than anybody in the world?" Moishele is asking the deepest question in the world — and in Heaven there's silence. The last Jewish child in the Warsaw ghetto is asking God the deepest question in the world. His father starts to answer, "*Avadim Hayinu*, we were slaves"; but the story is so long. This story has no end until Mashiach comes.

Then Moishele says, "*Tateh*, I have one more question of my own. Will you be alive at next year's Seder to answer me? Will I be alive next year to ask the *Mah Nishtanah*? Will any Jew be alive anywhere in the world to ask the *Mah Nishtanah*?" When he asked the first four questions there was silence in Heaven, but when Moishele asked his own question all the tears in Heaven were flowing. *HaKadosh baruch Hu* cried; the three fathers, the four mothers covered their faces and started crying. But Moishele's father — a *heilige Yid* — this is what he said: "*Ki v'sheim kodshecha nishbata lo*, by Your holy Name You swore to him *shelo yichbeh neiro l'olam va'ed*, that his lamp will never go out."

Moishele's father said to him, "I don't know if you'll be alive. I don't know if I'll be alive. But I know there will be one Moishele alive somewhere. There will still be a Moishele to ask the *Mah Nishtanah*, because the *Ribbono shel Olam*, the One, the only One, promised us there would always be one Moishele."

We were slaves

עבדים היינו

We tell our children that we were slaves but God took us out. I remember my father always telling us, "Imagine if we'd made a revolution." What if we

We were slaves to Pharaoh in Egypt, and Hashem our God took us out from there with a mighty hand and an outstretched arm. Had not the Holy One, blessed is He, taken our fathers out from Egypt, then we, our children, and our children's children would still be enslaved to Pharaoh in Egypt. And even if we were all wise, full of understanding, all elders and versed in the knowledge of Torah, it would still be our obligation to tell about the Exodus from Egypt. The more one dwells on the story of the Exodus, the more he is praiseworthy.

had come out of Egypt the way it happened in Russia? There the poor man made a revolution; so what did he do? He became the master, and he killed the rich man. First the rich man kills the poor, then the poor man kills the rich. That's not what happened with us; we became the servants of God. God uplifted us, so we came out of Egypt really free, from the deepest depths of our heart. The Talmud says that when we walked out of Egypt, we walked out like kings.

מַעֲשֶׂה בְּרַבִּי אֱלִיעֶזֶר וְרַבִּי יְהוֹשֻׁעַ וְרַבִּי אֶלְעָזָר בֶּן עֲזַרְיָה וְרַבִּי עֲקִיבָא וְרַבִּי טַרְפוֹן שֶׁהָיוּ מְסֻבִּין בִּבְנֵי בְרַק. וְהָיוּ מְסַפְּרִים בִּיצִיאַת מִצְרַיִם כָּל אוֹתוֹ הַלַּיְלָה. עַד שֶׁבָּאוּ תַלְמִידֵיהֶם וְאָמְרוּ לָהֶם. רַבּוֹתֵינוּ, הִגִּיעַ זְמַן קְרִיאַת שְׁמַע שֶׁל שַׁחֲרִית:

אָמַר רַבִּי אֶלְעָזָר בֶּן עֲזַרְיָה. הֲרֵי אֲנִי כְּבֶן שִׁבְעִים שָׁנָה, וְלֹא זָכִיתִי שֶׁתֵּאָמֵר יְצִיאַת מִצְרַיִם בַּלֵּילוֹת, עַד שֶׁדְּרָשָׁהּ בֶּן זוֹמָא, שֶׁנֶּאֱמַר, לְמַעַן תִּזְכֹּר אֶת יוֹם צֵאתְךָ מֵאֶרֶץ מִצְרַיִם כֹּל יְמֵי חַיֶּיךָ. יְמֵי חַיֶּיךָ הַיָּמִים, כֹּל יְמֵי חַיֶּיךָ הַלֵּילוֹת. וַחֲכָמִים אוֹמְרִים יְמֵי חַיֶּיךָ הָעוֹלָם הַזֶּה, כֹּל יְמֵי חַיֶּיךָ לְהָבִיא לִימוֹת הַמָּשִׁיחַ:

It happened...

מעשה

Rebbe Akiva lived in one the darkest periods in our history, after the destruction of our Temple. After Bar Cochba's uprising, which sadly enough didn't succeed, Rebbe Akiva wasn't allowed to learn Torah. The Jewish people didn't have any rights; they even had to hide being Jewish. But Rebbe Akiva sat all the night with Rebbe Yehoshua and Rebbe Tarfon. Can you see them telling us that the Redemption is coming?

It happened that Rabbi Eliezer, Rabbi Yehoshua, Rabbi Elazar ben Azaryah, Rabbi Akiva, and Rabbi Tarfon sat reclining at the Seder in Bnei Brak, and they discussed the story of the Exodus all that night, until their students came and said to them: "Our teachers, it is time for the reading of the morning Shema!"

Rabbi Elazar ben Azaryah said: I am like a seventy-year-old man, but I have not been privileged [on the basis of my opinion alone] to see the Exodus from Egypt mentioned every night, until Ben Zoma explained the verse "In order that you may remember the day you left Egypt all the days of your life." "The days of your life" would mean only the days; the additional word "all" includes the nights as well. But the Sages say that "the days of your life" would mean only the present world; the addition of "all" includes the days of Mashiach.

בָּרוּךְ הַמָּקוֹם, בָּרוּךְ הוּא. בָּרוּךְ שֶׁנָּתַן תּוֹרָה לְעַמּוֹ יִשְׂרָאֵל, בָּרוּךְ הוּא. כְּנֶגֶד אַרְבָּעָה בָנִים דִּבְּרָה תוֹרָה. אֶחָד חָכָם. וְאֶחָד רָשָׁע. וְאֶחָד תָּם. וְאֶחָד שֶׁאֵינוֹ יוֹדֵעַ לִשְׁאוֹל:

חָכָם מַה הוּא אוֹמֵר? מָה הָעֵדֹת וְהַחֻקִּים וְהַמִּשְׁפָּטִים אֲשֶׁר צִוָּה יְיָ אֱלֹהֵינוּ אֶתְכֶם? וְאַף אַתָּה אֱמָר לוֹ כְּהִלְכוֹת הַפֶּסַח, אֵין מַפְטִירִין אַחַר הַפֶּסַח אֲפִיקוֹמָן:

רָשָׁע מַה הוּא אוֹמֵר? מָה הָעֲבוֹדָה הַזֹּאת לָכֶם? לָכֶם - וְלֹא לוֹ. וּלְפִי שֶׁהוֹצִיא אֶת עַצְמוֹ מִן הַכְּלָל כָּפַר בְּעִקָּר, וְאַף אַתָּה הַקְהֵה אֶת שִׁנָּיו וֶאֱמָר לוֹ, בַּעֲבוּר זֶה עָשָׂה יְיָ לִי בְּצֵאתִי מִמִּצְרָיִם. לִי - וְלֹא לוֹ. אִלּוּ הָיָה שָׁם לֹא הָיָה נִגְאָל:

כנגד ארבעה בנים   **The Four Children**

It says in Tehillim, "*lehagid baboker chasdecha,* to tell Your kindness in the morning, *ve'emunascha baleilos,* and Your faith in the nights." To tell Your kindness — when the sun is shining, when things are good, it's not so hard to tell the world how beautiful God is. And your faith in the nights — what do you do when the night is so long? You just have to hold out and have faith.

There's a much deeper explanation by the Alexandrer Rebbe; I heard from his Chassidim that he said it in the Warsaw ghetto. This is what he said: "It doesn't say *emunasi,* my belief in You. That's not what gives me life at night. Instead it says *emunascha,* Your belief. The way God believes in us gives us life. When the night is so dark and endless, what keeps me alive is just remembering how much God believes in us. He believes that we will bring the coming day."

Blessed is God, blessed is He. Blessed is the One Who gave the Torah to His people Israel; blessed is He. Concerning four sons the Torah speaks: One who is wise, one who is wicked, one who is simple and one who does not know to ask.

The wise son – what does he say? "What is [the meaning of] the testimonies, decrees, and laws which Hashem, our God, has commanded us?" Therefore explain to him the laws of the Pesach offering: one may not eat dessert after the Pesach offering.

The wicked son – what does he say? "What [purpose] is this work to you?" He says, "to you", thereby excluding himself from the public. By excluding himself he denies the basic principle of our faith. Therefore you should blunt his teeth and say to him: "It is because of this [that we should serve Him in the future by refraining from chametz and eating matzah] that Hashem did [all these miracles] for me when I went out of Egypt." "For me," but not for him; had he been there, he would not have been redeemed.

Let me tell you about the four children. Some children are good, some are the best. Some are clever, and some are not so clever. Seder night gives me a taste of how much God believes in all of them. Sometimes you see young people that are a little "off." You know why they're off? Because there wasn't anybody to believe in them. It's so easy to get off the highway when nobody believes in you. Our holy Rabbis teach us that the *chacham*, the clever boy,

תָּם מַה הוּא אוֹמֵר? מַה זֹּאת? וְאָמַרְתָּ אֵלָיו בְּחֹזֶק יָד
הוֹצִיאָנוּ יְיָ מִמִּצְרַיִם מִבֵּית עֲבָדִים:

וְשֶׁאֵינוֹ יוֹדֵעַ לִשְׁאוֹל אַתְּ פְּתַח לוֹ. שֶׁנֶּאֱמַר וְהִגַּדְתָּ לְבִנְךָ
בַּיּוֹם הַהוּא לֵאמֹר בַּעֲבוּר זֶה עָשָׂה יְיָ לִי בְּצֵאתִי מִמִּצְרָיִם:

is very beautiful as long as you think that being clever is everything. The *chacham* is intellectual, he needs to be taught. How about stopping being only intellectual? How about tasting the *Afikoman*, tasting the depths of life, feeling deep emotion and serving God with it? The clever person isn't far away from the wicked person. Who do you think the wicked child is? Someone who was never told how holy he is.

Here's the most beautiful Belzer Torah. The Haggadah says, "When you talk to the wicked son blunt his teeth." It's a little heartbreaking — he came to the Seder, after all, and he didn't have to come at all. Now, the word רָשָׁע, "wicked," is made up of three letters. The outside letters are ר and ע, making רע, "bad"; but the inside letter is ש. And what does that mean? The three lines that make up a ש symbolize Avraham, Yitzchak, and Yaakov. If the *shin*, with its three lines, is on the inside of the *rasha*, that's to tell you that every Jew in the world is connected to our forefathers. His inside, his *neshamah*, is connected to them. So we tell the father, "blunt his teeth — *shinav*, his *shin*." If you want to educate this boy, knock his *shin* loose from the rest of him; bring out his inner nature, that's connected with the Fathers. Give him courage. Tell him not to make you think that he's not holy, because you know that he really is holy.

The *tam*, the simple child, is something different. The *tam* is just what his name says: he's perfect. He wants to know the deepest depths of everything.

In Hebrew there are two words for "this": *zeh* and *zos*. *Zeh* means something that you can point at, and *zos* means as if it's dark, but I know that the thing is there in the darkness. "Show me the deepest depths behind everything," says the *tam*. I tell him, "God will show it to you. God took us out of Egypt. There are certain deep lights that only God can give you."

The last son, the *she'eino yodeia lish'ol*, doesn't know how to ask a question. He's so glad to be alive, so glad to be a Jew. He says that he wants everything, but that even if he has nothing he's still so glad. *At p'sach lo*, "You open for him." God will open all the gates to him. Tonight He opens all the gates.

The simple son – what does he say? "What is this?" Tell him: "With a strong hand did Hashem take us out of Egypt, from the house of bondage."

As for the son who does not know to ask, you must open up for him, as it says: You shall tell your son on that day: "It is because of this [that we should serve Him in the future by refraining from chametz and eating matzah] that Hashem did [all these miracles] for me when I went out of Egypt."

My blessing for you is to make the Seder night exciting and beautiful. Let it be clear to you: on Seder night God is sending a message to parents, "It's in your hands; you are the parents, they're your children. Look at Me, look at God." What is God? A parent taking care of His children.

Sometimes our children are angry at us because we didn't give them enough courage. Sometimes they demand, "Why did you give us just words, why didn't you give us a taste of it?" The *rasha* asks, "Why didn't you ever tell me how holy I could be?" The *tam* says, "I'm so glad you taught me how perfect life is, how perfect *Yiddishkeit* is. But I don't want to go around thinking so simply, just thinking that everything is perfect and never knowing how or why. I want more than that." The *she'eino yodeia lish'ol* says, "Is *Yiddishkeit* a matter of always asking and begging, or is it something much deeper?" On Seder night we fix all of this. My blessing for you is to sit, husbands and wives and children together, with lots of *simchah*, and may you feel every second the deepest redemption.

יָכוֹל מֵרֹאשׁ חֹדֶשׁ, תַּלְמוּד לוֹמַר בַּיוֹם הַהוּא. אִי בַּיוֹם
הַהוּא יָכוֹל מִבְּעוֹד יוֹם, תַּלְמוּד לוֹמַר בַּעֲבוּר זֶה. בַּעֲבוּר זֶה
לֹא אָמַרְתִּי אֶלָּא בְּשָׁעָה שֶׁיֵּשׁ מַצָּה וּמָרוֹר מֻנָּחִים לְפָנֶיךָ:

מִתְּחִלָּה עוֹבְדֵי עֲבוֹדָה זָרָה הָיוּ אֲבוֹתֵינוּ, וְעַכְשָׁו קֵרְבָנוּ
הַמָּקוֹם לַעֲבוֹדָתוֹ. שֶׁנֶּאֱמַר, וַיֹּאמֶר יְהוֹשֻׁעַ אֶל כָּל הָעָם כֹּה
אָמַר יְיָ אֱלֹהֵי יִשְׂרָאֵל בְּעֵבֶר הַנָּהָר יָשְׁבוּ אֲבוֹתֵיכֶם מֵעוֹלָם,
תֶּרַח אֲבִי אַבְרָהָם וַאֲבִי נָחוֹר וַיַּעַבְדוּ אֱלֹהִים אֲחֵרִים. וָאֶקַּח
אֶת אֲבִיכֶם אֶת אַבְרָהָם מֵעֵבֶר הַנָּהָר וָאוֹלֵךְ אוֹתוֹ בְּכָל
אֶרֶץ כְּנָעַן וָאַרְבֶּה אֶת זַרְעוֹ וָאֶתֶּן לוֹ אֶת יִצְחָק. וָאֶתֵּן
לְיִצְחָק אֶת יַעֲקֹב וְאֶת עֵשָׂו וָאֶתֵּן לְעֵשָׂו אֶת הַר שֵׂעִיר
לָרֶשֶׁת אוֹתוֹ וְיַעֲקֹב וּבָנָיו יָרְדוּ מִצְרָיִם:

ואקח את אביכם   **And I took your father**

What's so special about Avraham Avinu coming to the Land of Israel? He
knew that this land becomes holy only when a Jew enters it. I'm this one Jew
coming into the Holy Land, and because of me it's becoming holy. In the
time of Avraham, why was it "the Holy Land"? Simply because Avraham was
there, even though he was the only one and there was nobody else there.
Imagine what would be if we all reached that level, where every *Yiddele*
knows that the Land is holy because of him.

One might think that from the beginning of the month there is an obligation to discuss the Exodus. [However,] it says [that you must tell your son] "on that day" (i.e., the day of Pesach). This could be understood to mean only during the daytime; therefore the Torah specifies, "it is because of this [that Hashem did for me when I went out of Egypt]." [The word "this" implies matzah and maror:] the commandment applies only when matzah and maror lie before you [at the Seder].

In early times our ancestors were idol worshipers, but now God has brought us closer to His service, as it says, "Yehoshua said to all the nation: 'So says Hashem, God of Israel: Your fathers always lived beyond the river, Terach the father of Avraham and the father of Nachor, and they served other gods. And I took your father Avraham from beyond the river and led him through all the land of Canaan. I increased his children and gave him Yitzchak. To Yitzchak I gave Yaakov and Eisav; to Eisav I gave Mount Seir to inherit, while Yaakov and his children went down to Egypt.'"

בָּרוּךְ שׁוֹמֵר הַבְטָחָתוֹ לְיִשְׂרָאֵל. בָּרוּךְ הוּא, שֶׁהַקָּדוֹשׁ
בָּרוּךְ הוּא חִשַּׁב אֶת הַקֵּץ לַעֲשׂוֹת כְּמָה שֶׁאָמַר לְאַבְרָהָם
אָבִינוּ בִּבְרִית בֵּין הַבְּתָרִים. שֶׁנֶּאֱמַר וַיֹּאמֶר לְאַבְרָם יָדֹעַ
תֵּדַע כִּי גֵר יִהְיֶה זַרְעֲךָ בְּאֶרֶץ לֹא לָהֶם וַעֲבָדוּם וְעִנּוּ אוֹתָם
אַרְבַּע מֵאוֹת שָׁנָה. וְגַם אֶת הַגּוֹי אֲשֶׁר יַעֲבֹדוּ דָּן אָנֹכִי
וְאַחֲרֵי כֵן יֵצְאוּ בִּרְכֻשׁ גָּדוֹל:

Cover the matzos, lift up the cup of wine, and say:

וְהִיא שֶׁעָמְדָה לַאֲבוֹתֵינוּ וְלָנוּ שֶׁלֹּא אֶחָד בִּלְבָד עָמַד
עָלֵינוּ לְכַלּוֹתֵנוּ אֶלָּא שֶׁבְּכָל דּוֹר וָדוֹר עוֹמְדִים עָלֵינוּ
לְכַלּוֹתֵנוּ וְהַקָּדוֹשׁ בָּרוּךְ הוּא מַצִּילֵנוּ מִיָּדָם:

ברוך שומר הבטחתו   **Blessed is He...**

You know, friends, sometimes we forget how much the *Ribbono shel Olam*
loves us, but then we remember and everything is good again. Sometimes we
forget that we have a covenant with God, the covenant He made with our
father Avraham. We forget that God can't achieve His purpose without the
Yidden and *Yidden* can't live without God. God's love towards us is infinite
— just remember, we have a covenant with God. In fact, every person has
two covenants: a private covenant and the covenant of all Israel. The
covenant gives you strength to hold out.

What does it mean to really have a covenant with God? Many people
think it means to be totally drunk on God. They're completely with God, but
they're not with the world. They don't see people any more, especially not
people who aren't believers just like them.

A person who has a real covenant with God has to be aware of every
little non-believer in the world. If Avraham hadn't welcomed in three angels,

Blessed is He Who keeps His promise to Israel; blessed is He! For the Holy One, blessed is He, calculated the end [of the days of slavery] in order to do as He said to our father Avraham at the Covenant between the Pieces, as it says: "He said to Avram, 'Know with certainty that your children will be aliens in a land that is not their own. They will serve them and they will oppress them four hundred years; but also upon the nation which they serve I will pass judgment, and afterwards they shall leave with great possessions.'"

Cover the matzos, lift up the cup of wine, and say:

And it is this promise which has sustained our fathers and us. For not only one enemy has risen against us to destroy us, but in every generation they rise against us to destroy us. But the Holy One, blessed is He, rescues us from their hand.

---

who were disguised as pagans, he would never have had Yitzchak, our holy forefather Isaac, and there would have been no hope for the world — because is there any existence for the world without God's children, the nation of Israel?

והיא שעמדה   And it is this promise

I was in Poland, where during the war thousands of Jewish children were put into non-Jewish homes. Their parents thought that after the war was over they'd come and pick up the children; but they never came. Those babies grew up. Even if they remembered that they were Jewish, there was nothing they could do about it.

They grew up, married *goyim,* had children. By now it's the second generation. Until a few years ago these children, now grown-up parents, never even told their own children that they were Jewish, but now, suddenly, *baruch Hashem,* an opening appears in the world. They start talking; they tell their children that they are Jewish. And now what? In Warsaw, in the big *shul* maybe twenty people pray. In Cracow, maybe fifteen people get together to *daven.* It's heartbreaking.

The greatest thing was when we went there and thousands of *goyim* came. Some were saying things like, "You know my mother is Jewish, my grandfather was Jewish." There was one boy — I can never forget him. I was walking in the streets of Biala, going to a concert, and I saw a sixteen-year-old boy wearing *tzitzis* and a cap. I spoke to him, and he spoke perfect Hebrew; I was sure he was from Israel. I said to him, "Where are you from, Yerushalayim the Holy City?" He said, "No, I'm from Cracow. I want you to know that two years ago I was on my *Zeide's* farm, where I go every summer. I went up in the attic, and I found a book there. It didn't look to me like English or German or Polish. I went over to Grandfather and asked him, 'What kind of book is this?' He got defensive and said, 'It's not my book.' I thought, 'What is he yelling about?' and left it alone. The next day I asked him, 'Why did you get so defensive about that book? What kind of book is it?' He looked at me, and then said, 'It's my *siddur,* and that's the truth.'"

This boy went and got himself tapes and dictionaries, and he learned Hebrew all by himself. Now he's wearing *tzitzis* and keeping kosher. Do you know what keeping kosher in Cracow means? This boy has nothing to eat. He lives on apples and potatoes — I couldn't believe it. What a *heilige neshamah!* We swore to him that we'd get him into a yeshivah in Eretz Yisrael.

What's so hard about being a *Yid* for me? Will I go to *Gan Eden* for eating kosher? I have a kosher grocery store next to me, a Meal Mart on the other corner, a *mikveh* half a block away. Why not?

I was invited to Warsaw by the art theater, to give a concert, and the greatest miracle happened. I arrived in Poland with about twenty people, and we were greeted by the television. We gave seven concerts. "Sold out" isn't the word — thousands of people came. People in the street greeted me with so much respect and *simchah.* You know, it's clear to me that if the *goyim* ever begin to love us, it'll only happen when they see a *Yid* with *pei'os* and a *yarmulke.*

Here's a very simple thing, and I'm sure you'll share my feelings about it. I'll explain to you with a parable. A young man is looking for a *shidduch*. He meets a young woman, and on the date she says to him, "Tell me about yourself." So he says, "I'll tell you. My first wife ran off after the *chuppah*. My second wife didn't even show up. The third wife I don't even remember." What does she do now? Is she going to think, "*Gevalt*, what a *shidduch*! When are we getting married?" No, she'll look at the clock and say, "*Oy vey*, I have a very important appointment."

This is *mamash* what we're doing to the world. Here's a new generation, and we come to them and we're saying, "This one wanted to kill us; this one killed us; this one is thinking of killing us." Imagine if I'm a little *goy*. I live in the big city, and I know nothing of *Yidden*; all I know is that everyone wants to kill them. There must be something wrong with them. And that is all we're talking about to our children!

Mamash for the first time, a Jew like me came to Poland. I didn't talk about anything bad, I just came and told them that I'm bringing regards from Yerushalayim.

I want you to know, God is opening gates for the whole world. We're the chosen people — let's not talk about killers. Are they what makes me a Jew? Do you think I'll bring peace into the world by telling my children about the Inquisition? Yes, I need to tell them a little, but do you know what I tell them? I say to them, "Can you imagine how holy these people were? God meant more to them than life!"

There's something that has kept us alive as Jews — the fact that someone is always coming to kill us, that keeps us alive. Sometimes we forget who we are, and sadly enough, there are some people who are against us. But it's clear to me that they're only messengers of God to let us know who we are — who I am — how holy it is to be a Jew.

I want to tell about two last wills: the dying words of two holy Jews. Here is one story:

"One night in Auschwitz my holy uncle woke me up from my sleep, and he said to me, 'You're going to be the only one left. Out of our whole family there's nobody left now but you and me, and I have a feeling that tonight is my last night. Tomorrow I'll walk with our father Yitzchak to the gas chambers. So you're the only one left, and I'm delivering my last will to you. This is my testament:

"'I want you to know that I've been three years in Auschwitz. I swear to you that I haven't stopped learning for one second. You know that I know most of the Talmud Bavli and Yerushalmi by heart. This morning I started *Mo'eid Katan* and tomorrow I'll be on the seventh page. If God blesses you and you come out of here alive, finish the tractate for me.'"

You see, my sweetest friends, the last wish of the six million is to finish all the tractates of the Talmud for them. Finish all the holy pages of all those holy *sefarim* that they never completed. What a will to give! My blessing to you is to pass it on to your children.

I heard the story of another last will. This story took place during the Six-Day War. I was giving a concert for thousands of soldiers, and the spirit was so high. Everyone was pouring out his heart, praying for the redemption of Israel. After the concert an officer came up to me and said,
"I want to tell you my story. I'm from a very left-wing kibbutz, and I didn't use to believe in God. I taught my children that religious people are fake, living in a world of lies. I told them that we Jews are the same as everyone else, and Israel is just as holy as Tokyo and Moscow.
"When the war began, I found myself fighting alongside an officer from a very religious kibbutz. Early in the morning, when the fighting began, he started shouting *Shema*. The whole time he was yelling at the top of his lungs. Eventually I said to him, 'Listen, my friend. I like you, but you're getting on my nerves. You know the way I feel about God. I can't stand this yelling all day about God. I know you believe in Him, I appreciate it, but please be quiet.'
"He just said to me, 'You have your way and I have mine.' By Thursday morning of the war I was already conditioned that my religious friend yelled *Shema Yisrael* constantly. That morning at dawn shooting began, but there was no yelling of *Shema Yisrael, Hashem Elokeinu, Hashem Echad.* I looked down at the ground and I saw that my *Yiddele* had been shot; he was dying. Blood was running out of his mouth, but he was still alive.
"Suddenly it was clear to me — *oy*, what a real Jew he is, how precious he is. I fell to the ground and I held his dying hand and I said, 'My dearest, sweetest brother, please forgive me for arguing with you all the time. Believe me, please: I wish I could die instead of you. Is there anything I can do for you?' He could hardly speak; I had to put my ear to his mouth. He said, 'Please promise me you'll say *Shema Yisrael* for me.' I said to him, 'I swear to you by the living God that for the rest of my life I'll say *Shema Yisrael* every day; and when I come back to my children, I'll teach them in your name to say *Shema Yisrael*.'"
That was the officer's story. He said to me, "You know, until then I didn't believe in God, but at that moment He opened the gates of Heaven for me. I don't just believe in God, I saw God. It was so clear that there is one God."

So you hear, my beautiful children — you know what you and I have to do. For all the holy soldiers who gave their lives for the Holy Land and for all the *Yidden* who died for God over the last two thousand years, we have to call out for them *Shema Yisrael*.

The cup is put down and the matzos uncovered.

צֵא וּלְמַד מַה בִּקֵשׁ לָבָן הָאֲרַמִּי לַעֲשׂוֹת לְיַעֲקֹב אָבִינוּ.
שֶׁפַּרְעֹה לֹא גָזַר אֶלָּא עַל הַזְּכָרִים וְלָבָן בִּקֵשׁ לַעֲקֹר אֶת
הַכֹּל. שֶׁנֶּאֱמַר אֲרַמִּי אֹבֵד אָבִי וַיֵּרֶד מִצְרַיְמָה וַיָּגָר שָׁם בִּמְתֵי
מְעָט, וַיְהִי שָׁם לְגוֹי גָּדוֹל עָצוּם וָרָב. וַיֵּרֶד מִצְרַיְמָה—אָנוּס
עַל פִּי הַדִּבּוּר. וַיָּגָר שָׁם —מְלַמֵּד שֶׁלֹּא יָרַד יַעֲקֹב אָבִינוּ
לְהִשְׁתַּקֵּעַ בְּמִצְרַיִם אֶלָּא לָגוּר שָׁם. שֶׁנֶּאֱמַר, וַיֹּאמְרוּ אֶל
פַּרְעֹה לָגוּר בָּאָרֶץ בָּאנוּ כִּי אֵין מִרְעֶה לַצֹּאן אֲשֶׁר לַעֲבָדֶיךָ,
כִּי כָבֵד הָרָעָב בְּאֶרֶץ כְּנָעַן, וְעַתָּה יֵשְׁבוּ נָא עֲבָדֶיךָ בְּאֶרֶץ
גֹּשֶׁן:

בקש לעקור את הכל Lavan attempted to uproot everything

Actually, it's impossible to uproot Yaakov Avinu. The special thing about Yaakov was that until he came into the world it was possible to fall away from *Yiddishkeit*. Avraham had a son, Yishmael, who stopped being Jewish, and he was lost. Yitzchak had Eisav, who did the same. But from the time Yaakov appeared, from then until the end of time, you can't stop being Jewish; nothing will do it. I always tell my friends, Imagine if the Pope was an apostate Jew. If he called R. Moshe Feinstein from Rome and asked if he was required to *bentsch* after his meals, R. Moshe would tell him, "Yes, of course you have to say the Grace after each meal." This guy is a converted Jew — he's the pope now — but all that doesn't matter. He's the same Jew that he always was. This isn't something within the framework of the world: it's *beini uvein bnei Yisrael*, between God and the children of Yaakov. It's so deep that nothing in the world can wipe it out.

When Eliezer, Avraham's servant, went to find a match for his master's son Yitzchak, he set himself a sign: "The first girl," he said, "that comes to the well and gives me and my camels to drink will be Yitzchak's wife." So Yitzchak met Rivkah and asked her for some water. Rivkah didn't just hear "Give me water," she understood what was inside the question: "Are you the wife of Yitzchak, the mother of Yaakov, the mother of *Yidden* who go to concentration camps for the sake of God, who are willing to die for God a

The cup is put down and the matzos uncovered.

Go and learn what Lavan the Aramean strove to do to our father Yaakov: for Pharaoh decreed [death] only for the males, but Lavan attempted to uproot everything, as it says: "An Aramean tried to destroy my father. Then he went down to Egypt and sojourned there with few people; and there he became a nation great, mighty and numerous."

He went down to Egypt – compelled by Divine decree. He sojourned there – this teaches that our father Yaakov did not go down to Egypt to settle there, but only to sojourn, as it says: "And they said to Pharaoh, 'We have come to sojourn in this land because there is no pasture for your servants' flocks, because the famine is severe in the land of Canaan. And now, please let your servants dwell in the land of Goshen.'"

---

thousand times? Do you have all that within you?" She answered back, "I have water for your camels too, for all the Jews until the end of the world."

בִּמְתֵי מְעָט כְּמָה שֶׁנֶּאֱמַר בְּשִׁבְעִים נֶפֶשׁ יָרְדוּ אֲבֹתֶיךָ
מִצְרָיְמָה וְעַתָּה שָׂמְךָ יְיָ אֱלֹהֶיךָ כְּכוֹכְבֵי הַשָּׁמַיִם לָרֹב. וַיְהִי
שָׁם לְגוֹי —מְלַמֵּד שֶׁהָיוּ יִשְׂרָאֵל מְצֻיָּנִים שָׁם. גָּדוֹל, עָצוּם
—כְּמָה שֶׁנֶּאֱמַר: וּבְנֵי יִשְׂרָאֵל פָּרוּ וַיִּשְׁרְצוּ וַיִּרְבּוּ וַיַּעַצְמוּ
בִּמְאֹד מְאֹד וַתִּמָּלֵא הָאָרֶץ אֹתָם. וָרָב — כְּמָה שֶׁנֶּאֱמַר:
רְבָבָה כְּצֶמַח הַשָּׂדֶה נְתַתִּיךְ וַתִּרְבִּי וַתִּגְדְּלִי וַתָּבֹאִי בַּעֲדִי
עֲדָיִים שָׁדַיִם נָכֹנוּ וּשְׂעָרֵךְ צִמֵּחַ וְאַתְּ עֵרֹם וְעֶרְיָה. וָאֶעֱבֹר
עָלַיִךְ וָאֶרְאֵךְ מִתְבּוֹסֶסֶת בְּדָמָיִךְ, וָאֹמַר לָךְ בְּדָמַיִךְ חֲיִי,
וָאֹמַר לָךְ בְּדָמַיִךְ חֲיִי:

בדמיך חיי   **Through your blood shall you live**

There was a Radomsker Chassid in Auschwitz, whose name was Reb
Naftali, and he did not give in. When Chanukkah was coming near he went
around telling everyone the last Torah thought the Radomsker Rebbe had
said before his death. The crux of the thought is that the light that is lit the
first night is the most important one. We even pray that it should last
forever, *shelo yichbeh neiro l'olam va'ed.*

The Nazis made it clear (as they did before every holiday) that anyone
caught lighting a candle would be shot on the spot. You can just imagine
what a person had to suffer to lay his hands on a candle in Auschwitz, let
alone that the Nazis were threatening death to anyone who did. But all the
yidden knew in their hearts that this Chassid would do anything to get hold
of a candle.

I'm sure you've heard that, in the camps, if someone showed up for the
morning roll-call not wearing shoes, he was punished with death. Well, late
one night, the first night of Chanukkah in fact, the *yidden* heard a scratching
at the door of their barracks. Reb Naftali walked in — without shoes on. But
more important to him, he was holding a candle in his hand. His shoes for
a Chanukkah candle: to him that was a fair trade.

All the *yidden* told him, "You don't have to risk your life for this mitzvah!
You know that if they don't kill you tonight, when they see you in the
morning they'll kill you instantly." Reb Naftali said to them, "But this is what

With few people – as it says: "With seventy souls your fathers went down to Egypt, and now Hashem, your God, has made you as numerous as the stars of heaven."

There he became a great nation – this teaches that the people of Israel were distinctive there.

Great, mighty – as it says: "And the Children of Israel were fruitful and increased and multiplied, and became mighty; and the land was filled with them."

And numerous – as it says: "I made you as numerous as the growth of the field; you multiplied, and became charming, with perfect breasts; and your hair has grown. But you remained naked and bare."

The Ari ל"ז adds this verse:

"And I passed over you and saw you wallowing in your blood, and I said to you, 'Through your blood shall you live!' And I said to you: 'Through your blood shall you live!'"

Chanukkah is all about: *mesirus nefesh*, risking your life for a single mitzvah." It was the first night of Chanukkah, and he had his mitzvah to do. That was all that mattered to him.

Reb Naftali went over to a small crack in the wall of the barracks, and that is where he put his candle, so everybody outside could see it burning. He lit the candle and said the blessing — and no more than two minutes later the guard burst in and started yelling, "Dirty Jews, who lit the candle?"

Reb Naftali said calmly, "It was me." Right away the Nazi started beating him, and ordered him to put out the flame. But Reb Naftali paid no attention. The whole time he just sang to himself "*haneiros hallalu*, we kindle these holy lights because of the miracles You did for our fathers." Needless

וַיָּרֵעוּ אֹתָנוּ הַמִּצְרִים וַיְעַנּוּנוּ וַיִּתְּנוּ עָלֵינוּ עֲבֹדָה קָשָׁה. וַיָּרֵעוּ
אֹתָנוּ הַמִּצְרִים—כְּמָה שֶׁנֶּאֱמַר: הָבָה נִתְחַכְּמָה לוֹ פֶּן יִרְבֶּה
וְהָיָה כִּי תִקְרֶאנָה מִלְחָמָה וְנוֹסַף גַּם הוּא עַל שֹׂנְאֵינוּ וְנִלְחַם
בָּנוּ וְעָלָה מִן הָאָרֶץ. וַיְעַנּוּנוּ—כְּמָה שֶׁנֶּאֱמַר: וַיָּשִׂימוּ עָלָיו
שָׂרֵי מִסִּים לְמַעַן עַנֹּתוֹ בְּסִבְלֹתָם וַיִּבֶן עָרֵי מִסְכְּנוֹת לְפַרְעֹה
אֶת פִּתֹם וְאֶת רַעַמְסֵס. וַיִּתְּנוּ עָלֵינוּ עֲבֹדָה קָשָׁה—כְּמָה
שֶׁנֶּאֱמַר: וַיַּעֲבִדוּ מִצְרַיִם אֶת בְּנֵי יִשְׂרָאֵל בְּפָרֶךְ:

to say, by the time the Nazi left Reb Naftali was at the brink of death. But lo and behold, the candle was still burning! Somehow the thug had not extinguished it before he left.

The next night the *yidden* could hardly believe their eyes. They just watched in astonishment as Reb Naftali, who was barely alive, limped over to the crack in the wall, pulled out another candle, and lit it.

ויעננו   **And they tormented us**

The night that Yitzchak blessed Yaakov was Seder night. Yitzchak saw that this night all the gates are open, so he could bless his son.

In Egypt we were on the lowest level you could imagine, as the Talmud says, that if we had stayed one more moment in Egypt, we would have been lost forever. But then the Seder night came, and all the gates opened. We got to the highest level in one second, and now we could leave Egypt. That's how it is: in order to be holy, usually you have to work on it for a whole lifetime; but on Seder night we say *Kaddesh*, make us holy, right now, tonight.

Yitzchak said to Yaakov, "*Mah zeh miharta limtzo*, how did you become so holy and uplifted so fast, that now you're worthy of receiving the blessings?" The Midrash says when Yaakov walked in to receive the blessing, Yitzchak saw Yosei of Shita. This Yosei was a traitor working with the Romans against his own Jewish brothers. When the Romans captured the

> "And the Egyptians did evil to us and tormented us and imposed hard labor upon us."
>
> The Egyptians did evil to us – as it says: "Come, let us deal wisely with them, lest they multiply, and then when a war breaks out they will join our enemies and fight against us, and escape from the land."
>
> And tormented us – as it says: "They set taskmasters over them in order to oppress them with their burdens, and they built Pisom and Raamses as treasure cities for Pharaoh."
>
> And imposed hard labor upon us – as it says: "The Egyptians enslaved the Children of Israel with hard work."

Temple, they ordered him to go in and be the first to desecrate the holy place. He did it, but when they ordered him to go back in, he refused: "It's enough that I've angered my Creator once," he said. The moment he walked into the Holy Temple, his soul caught on fire.

It's too gruesome to say what they did to him — enough to say they cut him in pieces. But he wouldn't defile his Holy Temple again, no matter what they did. This is what Yitzchak saw: that someone who was the lowest in the world could turn around to become so holy a moment later, and even though he was in so much pain he wouldn't give up his holiness again.

ויתנו עלינו עבודה קשה   They imposed hard labor upon us

We children of Avraham, Yitzchak, and Yaakov have two kinds of brothers and sisters. There are two kinds of *Yidden*, two kinds of holiness. There is the holiness of the Seer of Lublin, a prophet who learns Torah and fulfills every law — his whole life is spent serving God. And then there is

וַנִּצְעַק אֶל יְיָ אֱלֹהֵי אֲבֹתֵינוּ וַיִּשְׁמַע יְיָ אֶת קֹלֵנוּ וַיַּרְא אֶת
עָנְיֵנוּ וְאֶת עֲמָלֵנוּ וְאֶת לַחֲצֵנוּ. וַנִּצְעַק אֶל יְיָ אֱלֹהֵי אֲבֹתֵינוּ
כְּמָה שֶׁנֶּאֱמַר: וַיְהִי בַיָּמִים הָרַבִּים הָהֵם וַיָּמָת מֶלֶךְ מִצְרַיִם
וַיֵּאָנְחוּ בְנֵי יִשְׂרָאֵל מִן הָעֲבוֹדָה וַיִּזְעָקוּ וַתַּעַל שַׁוְעָתָם אֶל
הָאֱלֹהִים מִן הָעֲבוֹדָה. וַיִּשְׁמַע יְיָ אֶת קֹלֵנוּ   כְּמָה שֶׁנֶּאֱמַר:
וַיִּשְׁמַע אֱלֹהִים אֶת נַאֲקָתָם וַיִּזְכֹּר אֱלֹהִים אֶת בְּרִיתוֹ אֶת
אַבְרָהָם אֶת יִצְחָק וְאֶת יַעֲקֹב:

another holiness: a simple Jew, but a Jew who volunteers to take another
Jew's whipping, a Jew who willingly suffers instead of someone else. In the
Holy Land we have so many holy *Yidden*, great Kabbalists and scholars,
people who do mitzvos all day. And we also have so many unlearned *Yidden*
who are holy, too, like the holy soldiers, the holiest of the holy, the sweetest
of the sweet. What else can you say of someone who gives his life for you?
We pray for them: Master of the world, protect them, bring them back home
to us, answer their prayers.

ונצעק   We cried out

You know why we're never really happy nowadays? Because when we
have to cry, we don't really cry. We're living in a world where, from a certain
age on, you don't cry. What's wrong with crying?

We don't know how to cry. We don't know how to laugh. We don't laugh
out of joy any more. Children, when they cry, they cry, and when they laugh,
they laugh. Friends, I can only tell you: whenever you want to cry, cry with
all your heart. You know how much better you'll feel after you really cry? But
when you cry, do it before the One, the Only One — then suddenly great joy
from Heaven will descend into your heart.

> "We cried out to Hashem, the God of our fathers, and Hashem heard our voice and saw our affliction, our burden and our oppression."
>
> We cried out to Hashem, the God of our fathers – as it says: "And in the course of those many days the king of Egypt died, and the Children of Israel groaned amidst the work and screamed out; and their cry went up to God from the work."
>
> Hashem heard our voice – as it says: "God heard their moaning and God recalled His covenant with Avraham, with Yitzchak, and with Yaakov."

Tears flow up, not down. When you see someone's tears flowing down from their eyes, *gevalt*, they're really going up to Heaven.

When someone is crying, God gives you the greatest, deepest privilege: to kiss away their tears.

וישמע ה׳ את קולנו   **And Hashem heard our voice**

There is an awesome Torah in Parashas Vayeitzei. Yaakov Avinu was lying on the ground and dreaming: here is a ladder standing firmly on the ground and reaching upwards. Angels are going up and down. And the Torah says, *"v'hineih Hashem nitzav alav,* behold God is standing above him." The Izhbitzer Rebbe explains that there are two different words in Hebrew for "standing." There is *omeid,* which just means standing there, and there is *nitzav,* which means planted in place like a *matzeivah,* a gravestone — it has no choice, it can't move. A human being is always *omeid;* he can pick up his feet and walk away. A stone is only *nitzav.* So it was as if God said to Yaakov Avinu, "Do you think I have a choice not to be with you?" *V'hineih Hashem nitzav,* it was as if God was saying, "I have no choice."

Gevalt! This means that God was telling Yaakov, "You have a ladder, you

וַיַּרְא אֶת עָנְיֵנוּ—זוֹ פְּרִישׁוּת דֶּרֶךְ אֶרֶץ, כְּמָה שֶׁנֶּאֱמַר: וַיַּרְא
אֱלֹהִים אֶת בְּנֵי יִשְׂרָאֵל וַיֵּדַע אֱלֹהִים. וְאֶת עֲמָלֵנוּ — אֵלּוּ
הַבָּנִים, כְּמָה שֶׁנֶּאֱמַר: כָּל הַבֵּן הַיִּלּוֹד הַיְאֹרָה תַּשְׁלִיכֻהוּ וְכָל
הַבַּת תְּחַיּוּן. וְאֶת לַחֲצֵנוּ—זֶה הַדְּחַק, כְּמָה שֶׁנֶּאֱמַר: וְגַם
רָאִיתִי אֶת הַלַּחַץ אֲשֶׁר מִצְרַיִם לֹחֲצִים אֹתָם:

have the choice to go up and down. But I — it's as if I have no choice. I am always with you, I will always be there for you, because you are my child. I'll always love you, no matter where you are on the ladder, no matter what the situation."

And our oppression   וְאֶת לַחֲצֵנוּ

The Seer of Lublin, who lived one hundred years ago, was so holy that if someone who was sunk in materialism touched him, he couldn't bear it. That meant that when he needed a haircut, there could be complications. All the barbers in the city would work all week long on doing *teshuvah* and bringing out their Jewish purity and holiness, so that they would be pure enough to give the Rebbe a haircut, but they weren't always successful.

Once it was erev Shabbos and the Rebbe's hair needed cutting, and out of all the barbers in the city, there wasn't one who had really grown at all in purity that week. The Chassidim searched all around, and finally they found a "street barber," an itinerant who roamed from city to city finding work wherever he could. There wasn't anybody else, so they brought him before the Seer — who knew, maybe he was a *heiliger Yid* under his rags? Well, the moment this barber put his hands on the Rebbe's head, the Rebbe melted away with pleasure. He *mamash* enjoyed the haircut. So after the barber finished his job and they paid him, the Chassidim took him aside and asked him, "Who are you? *Gevalt*, are you holy!"

The barber didn't say anything; instead, he took off his shirt, and they saw that his whole body was full of the most terrible scars. The Chassidim asked where the scars were from. He told them, "You know that I'm just a street barber, and I wander from city to city looking for work. One time I walked into the market place of a city, and I heard a big commotion. A

> And saw our affliction – that is the separation of man and wife, as it says: "God saw the Children of Israel and God knew."
> And our burden – these are the sons, as it says: "Every son that is born you shall throw into the river, but every daughter you shall let live."
> And our oppression – this refers to the pressure [applied to the slave laborers], as it says: "And I have also seen the pressure with which the Egyptians are oppressing them."

woman and her children were crying and screaming.

"What was it all about? You know, in Russia, whenever a crime is done in the city, the police grab the nearest Jew and accuse him of the crime — it's easier than finding the real criminal. This is what I had walked in on. They had just grabbed a Jew and sentenced him to a hundred lashes, and his wife and children were screaming to Heaven about it.

"I looked over at the victim and I could see that he was going to die after seventy or seventy-five lashes. There was no way he could survive a hundred. So I went to the police and told them that I had done the crime. They didn't care one way or the other; they untied the *Yid* and told him he was free, there had been a 'mistake.' He ran over to his wife and children, and they were all crying. Meanwhile the police tied me up and began whipping me. I'm strong, I can take fifty lashes, but I figured that after much more than that I would die. So I started praying, 'Master of the world, I did it only for You. I don't know this Jew and he can't ever pay me back. Please save me.' Then I fainted, and when I woke up, the hundred lashes were over."

וַיּוֹצִיאֵנוּ יְיָ מִמִּצְרַיִם בְּיָד חֲזָקָה וּבִזְרֹעַ נְטוּיָה וּבְמֹרָא גָדֹל וּבְאֹתוֹת וּבְמֹפְתִים. וַיּוֹצִיאֵנוּ יְיָ מִמִּצְרַיִם—לֹא עַל יְדֵי מַלְאָךְ וְלֹא עַל יְדֵי שָׂרָף וְלֹא עַל יְדֵי שָׁלִיחַ אֶלָּא הַקָּדוֹשׁ בָּרוּךְ הוּא בִּכְבוֹדוֹ וּבְעַצְמוֹ, שֶׁנֶּאֱמַר: וְעָבַרְתִּי בְאֶרֶץ מִצְרַיִם בַּלַּיְלָה הַזֶּה וְהִכֵּיתִי כָל בְּכוֹר בְּאֶרֶץ מִצְרַיִם מֵאָדָם וְעַד בְּהֵמָה וּבְכָל אֱלֹהֵי מִצְרַיִם אֶעֱשֶׂה שְׁפָטִים אֲנִי יְיָ. וְעָבַרְתִּי בְאֶרֶץ מִצְרַיִם בַּלַּיְלָה הַזֶּה — אֲנִי וְלֹא מַלְאָךְ. וְהִכֵּיתִי כָל בְּכוֹר בְּאֶרֶץ מִצְרַיִם — אֲנִי וְלֹא שָׂרָף. וּבְכָל אֱלֹהֵי מִצְרַיִם אֶעֱשֶׂה שְׁפָטִים — אֲנִי וְלֹא הַשָּׁלִיחַ. אֲנִי יְיָ — אֲנִי הוּא וְלֹא אַחֵר:

It is I and no other   אני הוא ולא אחר

Everybody knows that when the Seder night comes, it becomes the holiest night of the year. There are other holy nights, but this one is right now, and now it's the holiest of all. Everybody's Seder, even one made by the most unlearned *Yid*, is accepted in Heaven in the deepest way. On Seder night, Heaven wakes up every Jewish heart. The lowest, most distant *Yiddele* feels so strongly Jewish, so holy, so redeemed and free.

On Shavuos God gave us the Torah; on Rosh Hashanah and Yom Kippur He forgives us; on Sukkos and Simchas Torah the *Ribbono shel Olam* gives us joy. But on Pesach the Master of the world reveals to every Jew that there is one God. "*Ani Hashem*, I and not an angel, I and not a messenger; I am Hashem and no one else." And the smallest, most unlearned little *Yiddele* — who knows how high he reaches on Seder night? We have no concept. It's totally beyond us.

One Seder night at the holy Rebbe Tzvi Elimelech's table, the Chassidim said to him at the end of the Seder, "Rebbe, nobody in the world makes a Seder like you." Rebbe Tzvi Elimelech said to them, "What do you know about Seders? Do you really want to know whose Seder reached the farthest to Heaven? Moishele the water carrier's Seder reached the highest."

The next morning, after *davening* was over, Rebbe Tzvi Elimelech said to

"Hashem brought us out of Egypt with a mighty hand and with an outstretched arm, and with great awe, and with signs and wonders."

Hashem brought us out of Egypt – not through an angel, not through a seraph, and not through a messenger; only the Holy One, blessed is He, in His glory, His own self, as it says: "I will pass through the land of Egypt on that night; I will smite all the firstborn in the land of Egypt from man to beast; and upon all the gods of Egypt I will execute judgment; I am Hashem." "I will pass through the land of Egypt on that night" – I and not an angel; "I will smite all the firstborn in the land of Egypt" – I and not a seraph; "and upon all the gods of Egypt I will execute judgment" – I and not a messenger; "I am Hashem" – it is I and no other.

the Chassidim, "Please bring Moishele the water carrier to me, and let him tell you what he did last night, how he conducted his Seder." The Chassidim went to Moishele and brought him before the holy Rebbe. The Rebbe said to him, "Moishele, tell us what you did last night at your Seder." Moishele the water carrier broke down in tears, totally broken, and said, "Rebbe, I promise you I'll never do it again. I promise you I'll never make such a Seder again."

But the *heilige* Rebbe Tzvi Elimelech was smiling. He said, "Moishele, Heaven forbid, I didn't bring you here to put you to shame. On the contrary, your Seder was so beautiful, I want you to tell us what you did."

He said, "Rebbe, you know I'm so poor that I have no joy in my life. The only thing I have is sometimes to get drunk; that's my only joy in life. But everybody knows that on Pesach you can't drink vodka, since it's made from grain, so I had a great idea. The night before Pesach I would drink all night, and then I'd be drunk all Pesach long. Now, Rebbe, I know that you're not permitted to drink vodka from ten minutes after nine in the morning, so in the morning, exactly ten minutes after nine, I stopped drinking. But *gevalt*, Rebbe, was I drunk! I was lying on my bed all day. In the evening my holy wife Chanele came to me and said, 'Moishele, aren't you ashamed before your children? Everybody in the world is making a Seder for his children, and your children have no Seder.' But I was so drunk I just said, 'Chanele, I wish I could suddenly not be drunk, but please let me sleep a little bit more.' Every fifteen minutes Chanele came and said, 'Moishele, please, the children are waiting for the Seder.' But I couldn't move.

"Finally my holy wife Chanele came in and said, 'Moishele, it's five minutes before dawn! In five minutes it'll be too late to make a Seder.' I used all my strength to get up. I made it to the table, and this is what I said: 'My sweet holy children, I want you to know I'm so ashamed of myself. Vodka can take away from me the power to give a Seder for my children. I swear to you I'll never drink again, just for my children's sake. But children, I want you to know what the Seder is all about. I want you to know there is one God. There is one God Who created the world. I want you to know that there is one God who chose Avraham, Yitzchak, and Yaakov. Then their children were slaves for two hundred and ten years in Egypt. They were crying; their lives were so full of pain, it was unbearable. They prayed to the Only One, and the Master of the world heard their prayers. Tonight of all nights He took us out of Egypt. Children, swear to me, swear to me tonight that you'll never forget there is one God Who listens to all our prayers. Children, make sure you never stop praying.' That's all I said, and then I fell asleep again."

Rebbe Tzvi Elimelech was crying and crying. He said to the Chassidim, "Did you hear what kind of Seder Moishele gave? I wish that once in my life I could get it across to my children the way Moishele the water carrier did that there is one God."

Ani Hashem v'lo acheir. There is only one.

אני ה׳ ... ולא אחר   I am Hashem... and no other

These few words give us the whole message of the Haggadah. This is what it was all about, going out from Egypt: believing in one God, just the Only One. What does it mean to believe? Rebbe Nachman explains: There are two kinds of knowledge in the world — they're so different they're almost like two worlds. There is *emes*, truth, and then there is *emunah*, believing. It's not that the things we believe in aren't the truth; it's that belief is so much deeper than just truth. Because truth is just things that we know, things that we can figure out, things that can be understood and proven. But that sort of thing is so limited; and that's where faith begins. It begins where knowing the truth leaves off. Belief is so much deeper — I can't prove it, but I know it's the truth. It's an extension, it goes past what knowledge can do, it's something that goes beyond knowing. You know, it's like a beautiful song: I can sit here describing it all day, but really it's beyond my power to describe. Beyond what I can tell you lies so much more — *gevalt,* is it deep! My blessing for you is that you'll be able to pass on to your children the belief in the One, the only One. It's the best thing in the world for them to have, because with belief we can survive all the tornadoes of the world.

When everything looks wrong to us; when the house is falling apart; when the house has already collapsed; when someone has just died — what do we do then? We get up and yell, *"Yisgadal v'yiskadash shmeih rabba!* God's name is great; everything is still good." You know, my sweet friends, we can really say that, because in the deepest, most inside part of us, we know that Hashem is taking care of the world. And even if we don't know what's going on just now, we believe it's for the good, we believe it will be good in the end; and believing is so much more than knowing.

בְּיָד חֲזָקָה — זוֹ הַדֶּבֶר, כְּמָה שֶׁנֶּאֱמַר: הִנֵּה יַד יְיָ הוֹיָה
בְּמִקְנְךָ אֲשֶׁר בַּשָּׂדֶה בַּסּוּסִים בַּחֲמֹרִים בַּגְּמַלִּים בַּבָּקָר
וּבַצֹּאן דֶּבֶר כָּבֵד מְאֹד. וּבִזְרֹעַ נְטוּיָה — זוֹ הַחֶרֶב, כְּמָה
שֶׁנֶּאֱמַר: וְחַרְבּוֹ שְׁלוּפָה בְּיָדוֹ נְטוּיָה עַל יְרוּשָׁלָיִם. וּבְמֹרָא
גָדֹל — זֶה גִּלּוּי שְׁכִינָה, כְּמָה שֶׁנֶּאֱמַר: אוֹ הֲנִסָּה אֱלֹהִים
לָבוֹא לָקַחַת לוֹ גּוֹי מִקֶּרֶב גּוֹי בְּמַסֹּת בְּאֹתֹת וּבְמוֹפְתִים
וּבְמִלְחָמָה וּבְיָד חֲזָקָה וּבִזְרוֹעַ נְטוּיָה וּבְמוֹרָאִים גְּדֹלִים כְּכֹל
אֲשֶׁר עָשָׂה לָכֶם יְיָ אֱלֹהֵיכֶם בְּמִצְרַיִם לְעֵינֶיךָ. וּבְאֹתוֹת —
זֶה הַמַּטֶּה, כְּמָה שֶׁנֶּאֱמַר: וְאֶת הַמַּטֶּה הַזֶּה תִּקַּח בְּיָדֶךָ
אֲשֶׁר תַּעֲשֶׂה בּוֹ אֶת הָאֹתֹת. וּבְמֹפְתִים — זֶה הַדָּם, כְּמָה
שֶׁנֶּאֱמַר: וְנָתַתִּי מוֹפְתִים בַּשָּׁמַיִם וּבָאָרֶץ:

Remove one drop of wine for each of the three calamities:

דָּם, וָאֵשׁ, וְתִימְרוֹת עָשָׁן:

באותות **With signs**

Everybody likes it when God does miracles for him. The question is, do
you understand that you are a miracle, that your life is all miracles, that
everything is a miracle? If you're living on the level where miracles are part
of your life, if your trust in God reaches the level of a miracle, then miracles
happen to you. If you're not living life on that level, then miracles won't
happen to you.

With a mighty hand – this refers to the pestilence, as it says: "The hand of Hashem will strike your livestock which are in the field – the horses, the donkeys, the camels, the oxen, and the sheep – with a very severe pestilence."

And with an outstretched arm – this refers to the sword, as it says: "His sword is drawn in His hand, outstretched over Jerusalem."

And with great awe – this refers to the revelation of the Divine Presence, as it says: "Has God ever tried to take unto Himself one nation from the midst of another nation, with trials, miraculous signs, and wonders, with war, with a mighty hand and an out-stretched arm, and with awesome revelations, like all that Hashem your God did for you in Egypt, before your eyes?"

And with signs – this refers to the rod, as it says: "Take this rod in your hand, with which you will perform the miraculous signs."

And with wonders – this refers to the blood, as it says: "And I will show wonders in the heavens and on the earth:

Remove one drop of wine for each of the three calamities:

"Blood, fire, and columns of smoke."

דָּבָר אַחֵר בְּיָד חֲזָקָה שְׁתַּיִם. וּבִזְרוֹעַ נְטוּיָה שְׁתַּיִם. וּבְמוֹרָא גָדוֹל שְׁתַּיִם. וּבְאֹתוֹת שְׁתַּיִם. וּבְמוֹפְתִים שְׁתַּיִם.

אֵלּוּ עֶשֶׂר מַכּוֹת שֶׁהֵבִיא הַקָּדוֹשׁ בָּרוּךְ הוּא עַל הַמִּצְרִים בְּמִצְרַיִם. וְאֵלּוּ הֵן

As each of the plagues is mentioned, a drop of wine is removed from the cup.

כִּנִּים	צְפַרְדֵּעַ	דָּם
שְׁחִין	דֶּבֶר	עָרוֹב
חֹשֶׁךְ	אַרְבֶּה	בָּרָד
	מַכַּת בְּכוֹרוֹת	

Remove 3 drops of wine for each abbreviation.

רַבִּי יְהוּדָה הָיָה נוֹתֵן בָּהֶם סִימָנִים

דְּצַ"ךְ עֲדַ"שׁ בְּאַחַ"ב:

רַבִּי יוֹסֵי הַגְּלִילִי אוֹמֵר מִנַּיִן אַתָּה אוֹמֵר שֶׁלָּקוּ הַמִּצְרִים בְּמִצְרַיִם עֶשֶׂר מַכּוֹת וְעַל הַיָּם לָקוּ חֲמִשִּׁים מַכּוֹת. בְּמִצְרַיִם מַה הוּא אוֹמֵר, וַיֹּאמְרוּ הַחַרְטֻמִּם אֶל פַּרְעֹה אֶצְבַּע אֱלֹהִים הוּא. וְעַל הַיָּם מָה הוּא אוֹמֵר, וַיַּרְא יִשְׂרָאֵל אֶת הַיָּד הַגְּדֹלָה אֲשֶׁר עָשָׂה יְיָ בְּמִצְרַיִם וַיִּירְאוּ הָעָם אֶת יְיָ וַיַּאֲמִינוּ בַּייָ וּבְמֹשֶׁה עַבְדּוֹ. כַּמָּה לָקוּ בְּאֶצְבַּע עֶשֶׂר מַכּוֹת. אֱמֹר מֵעַתָּה, בְּמִצְרַיִם לָקוּ עֶשֶׂר מַכּוֹת וְעַל הַיָּם לָקוּ חֲמִשִּׁים מַכּוֹת.

Another interpretation of the preceding verse: With a mighty hand — two (plagues). And with an out-stretched arm — two. And with great awe — two. And with signs — two. And with wonders — two. These are the ten plagues which the Holy One, blessed is He, brought on the Egyptians in Egypt:

As each of the plagues is mentioned, a drop of wine is removed from the cup.

Blood	Frogs	Vermin
Wild Beasts	Pestilence	Boils
Hail	Locusts	Darkness
	Slaying of the Firstborn	

Remove 3 drops of wine for each abbreviation.

Rabbi Yehudah abbreviated them by their initials:
D'tzach, Adash, B'achav

Rabbi Yosei the Galilean said: From where can one deduce that the Egyptians suffered ten plagues in Egypt, but fifty plagues at the sea? About the plagues in Egypt what does it say? "The magicians said to Pharaoh, 'It is the finger of God.'" But of the events at the sea the Torah says: "Israel saw the great hand which Hashem laid upon the Egyptians, and the people feared Hashem and they believed in Hashem and in His servant Moshe." How many plagues did the Egyptians receive from one finger? Ten. From here we conclude that if they suffered ten plagues in Egypt they suffered fifty at the sea.

רַבִּי אֱלִיעֶזֶר אוֹמֵר מִנַּיִן שֶׁכָּל מַכָּה וּמַכָּה שֶׁהֵבִיא הַקָּדוֹשׁ בָּרוּךְ הוּא עַל הַמִּצְרִים בְּמִצְרַיִם הָיְתָה שֶׁל אַרְבַּע מַכּוֹת. שֶׁנֶּאֱמַר יְשַׁלַּח בָּם חֲרוֹן אַפּוֹ עֶבְרָה וָזַעַם וְצָרָה מִשְׁלַחַת מַלְאֲכֵי רָעִים. עֶבְרָה אַחַת. וָזַעַם שְׁתַּיִם. וְצָרָה שָׁלוֹשׁ. מִשְׁלַחַת מַלְאֲכֵי רָעִים אַרְבַּע. אֱמֹר מֵעַתָּה בְּמִצְרַיִם לָקוּ אַרְבָּעִים מַכּוֹת וְעַל הַיָּם לָקוּ מָאתַיִם מַכּוֹת.

רַבִּי עֲקִיבָא אוֹמֵר מִנַּיִן שֶׁכָּל מַכָּה וּמַכָּה שֶׁהֵבִיא הַקָּדוֹשׁ בָּרוּךְ הוּא עַל הַמִּצְרִים בְּמִצְרַיִם הָיְתָה שֶׁל חָמֵשׁ מַכּוֹת. שֶׁנֶּאֱמַר יְשַׁלַּח בָּם חֲרוֹן אַפּוֹ עֶבְרָה וָזַעַם וְצָרָה מִשְׁלַחַת מַלְאֲכֵי רָעִים. חֲרוֹן אַפּוֹ אַחַת. עֶבְרָה שְׁתַּיִם. וָזַעַם שָׁלֹשׁ. וְצָרָה אַרְבַּע. מִשְׁלַחַת מַלְאֲכֵי רָעִים חָמֵשׁ. אֱמֹר מֵעַתָּה בְּמִצְרַיִם לָקוּ חֲמִשִּׁים מַכּוֹת וְעַל הַיָּם לָקוּ חֲמִשִּׁים וּמָאתַיִם מַכּוֹת.

כַּמָּה מַעֲלוֹת טוֹבוֹת לַמָּקוֹם עָלֵינוּ

Rabbi Eliezer said: How does one know that every plague that the Holy One, blessed is He, brought upon the Egyptians in Egypt was composed of four elements of plague? For it says: "He sent upon them his fierce anger: wrath, fury, and trouble, a team of hostile angels." Wrath is one, fury is two, trouble is three, and a team of hostile angels is four. From here we can conclude that in Egypt they were struck by forty plagues [each of the ten having these four elements], and at the Sea they were struck with two hundred plagues.

Rabbi Akiva said: How does one know that each plague that the Holy One, blessed is He, brought upon the Egyptians in Egypt was composed of five elements of plague? For it says: "He sent upon them His fierce anger, wrath, fury, trouble, and a team of hostile angels." Fierce anger is one, wrath is two, fury is three, trouble is four and a team of hostile angels is five. From here we can conclude that in Egypt they were struck by fifty plagues and by the Sea two hundred and fifty.

So many favors has God bestowed upon us!

אִלּוּ הוֹצִיאָנוּ מִמִּצְרַיִם

וְלֹא עָשָׂה בָהֶם שְׁפָטִים דַּיֵּנוּ:

אִלּוּ עָשָׂה בָהֶם שְׁפָטִים

וְלֹא עָשָׂה בֵאלֹהֵיהֶם דַּיֵּנוּ:

אִלּוּ עָשָׂה בֵאלֹהֵיהֶם

וְלֹא הָרַג אֶת בְּכוֹרֵיהֶם דַּיֵּנוּ:

אִלּוּ הָרַג אֶת בְּכוֹרֵיהֶם

וְלֹא נָתַן לָנוּ אֶת מָמוֹנָם דַּיֵּנוּ:

אִלּוּ נָתַן לָנוּ אֶת מָמוֹנָם

וְלֹא קָרַע לָנוּ אֶת הַיָּם דַּיֵּנוּ:

אִלּוּ קָרַע לָנוּ אֶת הַיָּם

וְלֹא הֶעֱבִירָנוּ בְּתוֹכוֹ בֶּחָרָבָה דַּיֵּנוּ:

אִלּוּ הֶעֱבִירָנוּ בְּתוֹכוֹ בֶּחָרָבָה

וְלֹא שִׁקַּע צָרֵינוּ בְּתוֹכוֹ דַּיֵּנוּ:

אִלּוּ שִׁקַּע צָרֵינוּ בְּתוֹכוֹ

וְלֹא סִפֵּק צָרְכֵּנוּ בַּמִּדְבָּר אַרְבָּעִים שָׁנָה דַּיֵּנוּ:

אִלּוּ סִפֵּק צָרְכֵּנוּ בַּמִּדְבָּר אַרְבָּעִים שָׁנָה

וְלֹא הֶאֱכִילָנוּ אֶת הַמָּן דַּיֵּנוּ:

אִלּוּ הֶאֱכִילָנוּ אֶת הַמָּן

וְלֹא נָתַן לָנוּ אֶת הַשַּׁבָּת דַּיֵּנוּ:

Had He brought us out of Egypt, and not executed judgment against the Egyptians, it would have been enough for us.

Had he executed judgment against them, and not on their gods, it would have been enough for us.

Had He executed judgment against their gods, and not slain their firstborn, it would have been enough for us.

Had He slain their firstborn, and not given us their wealth, it would have been enough for us.

Had He given us their wealth, and not split the sea for us, it would have been enough for us.

Had He split the sea for us, and not led us through it on dry land, it would have been enough for us.

Had He led us through on dry land, and not drowned our tormentors in it, it would have been enough for us.

Had He drowned our tormentors in it, and not provided for our needs in the desert for forty years, it would have been enough for us.

Had He provided for our needs in the desert for forty years, and not fed us the manna, it would have been enough for us.

Had he fed us the manna, and not given us the Shabbos, it would have been enough for us.

אִלּוּ נָתַן לָנוּ אֶת הַשַּׁבָּת
דַּיֵּנוּ: וְלֹא קֵרְבָנוּ לִפְנֵי הַר סִינַי
אִלּוּ קֵרְבָנוּ לִפְנֵי הַר סִינַי
דַּיֵּנוּ: וְלֹא נָתַן לָנוּ אֶת הַתּוֹרָה
אִלּוּ נָתַן לָנוּ אֶת הַתּוֹרָה
דַּיֵּנוּ: וְלֹא הִכְנִיסָנוּ לְאֶרֶץ יִשְׂרָאֵל
אִלּוּ הִכְנִיסָנוּ לְאֶרֶץ יִשְׂרָאֵל
וְלֹא בָנָה לָנוּ אֶת בֵּית הַבְּחִירָה דַּיֵּנוּ:

Had He given us the Shabbos   אילו נתן לנו את השבת

You can keep every Shabbos according to the letter of the law, and all the same you haven't kept Shabbos yet. Unless Shabbos reaches the highest, deepest place in your heart, you haven't felt it yet. What is the highest place in your heart? Where it touches you the deepest. *Kosveim al luach libecha*, it should be written on your heart, "I realize that I can never do without it. I can't live without it."

The Talmud says that the *heilige* Shabbos is a gift from Heaven. The sweetness of Shabbos, the *oneg Shabbos*, the holiness of Shabbos — you have to ask for these. You have to pray that Hashem should give you Shabbos, because we need it so much.

We too, we have the power, God gave us the strength to make Shabbos so holy, so beautiful. We all would like everyone in the Holy Land to have Shabbos, but to do that we have to pray that Hashem should give us all the gift of Shabbos, and we have to give each other the gift of Shabbos. We have to make our Shabbos so sweet that everybody wants a piece of it. This is the meaning of *am mekadshei shevi'i*, the people that makes Shabbos holy.

My blessing to you and to me is that we should give Shabbos to our children, to our neighbors. Maybe one day the whole world will be full of Shabbos, the bliss, the sweetness of the *yom shekulo Shabbos*, the day that's all Shabbos. The whole world will be Shabbos.

> Had He given us the Shabbos, and not brought us before Mount Sinai, it would have been enough for us.
>
> Had He brought us before Mount Sinai, and not given us the Torah, it would have been enough for us.
>
> Had He given us the Torah, and not brought us into the Land of Israel, it would have been enough for us.
>
> Had He brought us into the Land of Israel, and not built the Holy Temple for us, it would have been enough for us.

Rebbe Nachman says, "Do you know why there is no peace in the world? Because you can only make peace when you're full of joy." You can't make peace when you have anger in you — anger doesn't make peace. *Shabbos shalom umevorach;* only with Shabbos, with sweetness and holiness can we bring peace to the world.

אילו נתן לנו את התורה   Had He given us the Torah

It says *"ki heim chayeinu,* the Torah is our life and our length of days, and we will study it day and night." Every night before a *Yid* goes to sleep he reminds himself what it means to be a *Yid*.

And what is a *Yid*? The Gemara says that there are people who eat bread just for the sake of more bread. You meet a person on the street and ask him, "Why do you eat?" He'll say, "In order to have strength." "Why do you need strength?" "In order to work." "Why do you work?" "In order to make money. You need money to buy bread." Why do you need bread? So you can work for bread? It's bread for bread and nothing else. I hate to say it, but this is most of the world.

Now, if you ask a little *Yiddele,* "What are you eating for?" he'll tell you,

עַל אַחַת כַּמָּה וְכַמָּה טוֹבָה כְפוּלָה וּמְכֻפֶּלֶת לַמָּקוֹם עָלֵינוּ.
שֶׁהוֹצִיאָנוּ מִמִּצְרַיִם. וְעָשָׂה בָהֶם שְׁפָטִים. וְעָשָׂה
בֵאלֹהֵיהֶם. וְהָרַג אֶת בְּכוֹרֵיהֶם. וְנָתַן לָנוּ אֶת מָמוֹנָם. וְקָרַע
לָנוּ אֶת הַיָּם. וְהֶעֱבִירָנוּ בְתוֹכוֹ בֶּחָרָבָה. וְשִׁקַּע צָרֵינוּ בְּתוֹכוֹ.
וְסִפֵּק צָרְכֵנוּ בַּמִּדְבָּר אַרְבָּעִים שָׁנָה. וְהֶאֱכִילָנוּ אֶת הַמָּן.
וְנָתַן לָנוּ אֶת הַשַּׁבָּת. וְקֵרְבָנוּ לִפְנֵי הַר סִינַי. וְנָתַן לָנוּ אֶת
הַתּוֹרָה. וְהִכְנִיסָנוּ לְאֶרֶץ יִשְׂרָאֵל. וּבָנָה לָנוּ אֶת בֵּית
הַבְּחִירָה לְכַפֵּר עַל כָּל עֲווֹנוֹתֵינוּ:

"In order to have strength to serve God, to be a *Yid*, to make the world better." And that's just the lower type of *Yiddele*. There's also a higher type, who doesn't even live on bread and water. You ask him what he's living on and he says, *"Ki heim chayeinu — Torah is my life. I'm living on learning and praying, on being a Jew. My very life depends on it."*

There is a story in *Tanna d'Vei Eliyahu*. Elijah the Prophet walked the streets of the world, and one night he met a little fisherman on the street. He asked him, "Have you studied the Torah? Have you studied the five books of Moses? Have you studied the Talmud? Have you studied the mysteries of the world?" The little fisherman's eyes began to shimmer with tears and he said, "Believe me, my holy prophet, I have tried so hard, I have tried so long. But the Almighty has not blessed me with a mind to fathom His holy teachings." Eliyahu Hanavi asked him, "Tell me, little fisherman, are you good at your trade?" His eyes glowed with pride and he said, "Holy prophet, believe me, I'm the best fisherman on this entire coast." Elijah began to cry and told him, "Do you know why you're the best fisherman in the region? Because you know that your life depends on fishing. If you only knew that your life depends on learning, you'd be the greatest scholar in the region."

Imagine if I knew the Torah was given only to me, all its holiness was made just for me — how I would throw myself at every word! How I would cry over every word to understand it! When I receive a letter from someone

> How much more, then, multiplied, doubled, and
> redoubled, are the favors that God has showered
> upon us; for He brought us out of Egypt; and execut-
> ed judgment against them and against their gods;
> and slew their firstborn; and gave us their wealth;
> and split the sea for us; and led us through it on dry
> land; and drowned our tormentors in it; and provided
> for our needs in the desert for forty years; and fed us
> the manna; and gave us the Shabbos; and brought us
> before Mount Sinai; and gave us the Torah; and
> brought us to the Land of Israel; and built us the
> Holy Temple, to atone for our sins.

I love I can't stop reading. This is how we have to learn Torah, as a love-letter from God to us.

Had He brought us in   אילו הכניסנו

When Hashem created the world, He stood in Eretz Yisrael, in Yerushala-yim, and from there He created the world. Do you know why Moshe Rabbe-nu, our holy leader, died? Because he didn't go to Eretz Yisrael. Moshe Rabbenu brought down into the world the reality that unless I go to the Holy Land I can't live.

When the Jews walked into Eretz Yisrael in the time of Yehoshua, it was all the Jews together. But Avraham Avinu, when God gave him the Land, was *mamash* the one Jew, who went in all by himself. All the holiness was for him alone.

Later on Moshe Rabbenu stood alone on the mountaintop, seeing the Holy Land all by himself. Seeing the Land was another great thing that he accomplished. Many people live in Israel, but don't see the Land any more.

Replace the wine that was removed during the recital of the plagues.

רַבָּן גַּמְלִיאֵל הָיָה אוֹמֵר כָּל שֶׁלֹּא אָמַר שְׁלֹשָׁה דְבָרִים אֵלּוּ
בַּפֶּסַח לֹא יָצָא יְדֵי חוֹבָתוֹ. וְאֵלּוּ הֵן:

פֶּסַח מַצָה וּמָרוֹר

We look at the shank-bone and recite the following:

פֶּסַח שֶׁהָיוּ אֲבוֹתֵינוּ אוֹכְלִים בִּזְמַן שֶׁבֵּית הַמִּקְדָּשׁ הָיָה קַיָּם
עַל שׁוּם מָה. עַל שׁוּם שֶׁפָּסַח הַקָּדוֹשׁ בָּרוּךְ הוּא עַל בָּתֵּי
אֲבוֹתֵינוּ בְּמִצְרַיִם שֶׁנֶּאֱמַר וַאֲמַרְתֶּם זֶבַח פֶּסַח הוּא לַיְיָ אֲשֶׁר
פָּסַח עַל בָּתֵּי בְנֵי יִשְׂרָאֵל בְּמִצְרַיִם בְּנָגְפּוֹ אֶת מִצְרַיִם וְאֶת
בָּתֵּינוּ הִצִּיל וַיִּקֹּד הָעָם וַיִּשְׁתַּחֲווּ:

You know what happens — many people come there and they get swallowed up by little details until they don't see the big picture any more. They don't see the Land any more. But then, there are many people who see the Land all the time even though they're not there.

The difference between *Yidden* and the world is like this. Take a German: when he's in Germany, he lives there — it's his home. If he lives somewhere else, that's his home now, and Germany doesn't matter any more to him. With the *Yidden*, however, between us and Eretz Yisrael there's an unbreakable connection. We couldn't be there for two thousand years, but we're still connected, because God brought us in there.

עַל אַחַת כַּמָּה וְכַמָּה   **How much more**

We left Egypt and we think we're free. You know what's so beautiful about it? On this first night of freedom I'm free inside. Inside I know there's one God, even though I didn't actually walk out of Egypt. I'm sitting with my family the whole night, with my children.

When we walked out of Egypt we weren't free yet. We were still afraid of

Replace the wine that was removed during the recital of the plagues.

Rabban Gamliel used to say: "Whoever does not say these three things on Passover has not fulfilled his duty, and these are they:

Pesach, Matzah, and Maror."

We look at the shank-bone and recite the following:

The Pesach offering which our fathers ate during the period of the Holy Temple – what is its meaning? It is because the Holy One, blessed is He, passed over our fathers' houses in Egypt, as it says: "You shall say, 'It is a Pesach offering for Hashem, Who passed over the houses of the Children of Israel in Egypt when He smote the Egyptians and spared our houses.' And the nation bowed down and prostrated themselves."

Pharaoh. After six days Pharaoh came running after us to bring us back, and the Torah says we were afraid. Here we are at the great moment: we're crossing the Red Sea and Pharaoh is drowning. We see with our eyes not to be afraid of Pharaoh — he has no dominion over us. Friends, what we and Israel need most is not to be afraid of the world any more. God is the king of the world, the master.

The *heilige* Izhbitzer Rebbe teaches us why the Red Sea became dry land for us. The sea looked at us *Yidden*, who were slaves for two hundred and ten years, and six nights later we're standing by the shores of the Red Sea. *Gevalt*, have we changed! In one week we've reached the highest of levels. By *Shevi'i shel Pesach*, the seventh day of Pesach, we were ready to dance through all the obstacles, all the oceans, winds, and tornadoes in the world. The sea took a look and said, "For their sake I will change too."

You can see the holiness of *Yidden* in the fact that for the sake of God we can change in one second. For our families, too, we can change instantly. The Talmud says that getting married is like crossing the Red Sea. The

Lift up the matzah and recite the following:

מַצָּה זוֹ שֶׁאָנוּ אוֹכְלִים עַל שׁוּם מָה. עַל שׁוּם שֶׁלֹּא הִסְפִּיק בְּצֵקָם שֶׁל אֲבוֹתֵינוּ לְהַחֲמִיץ עַד שֶׁנִּגְלָה עֲלֵיהֶם מֶלֶךְ מַלְכֵי הַמְּלָכִים הַקָּדוֹשׁ בָּרוּךְ הוּא וּגְאָלָם. שֶׁנֶּאֱמַר וַיֹּאפוּ אֶת הַבָּצֵק אֲשֶׁר הוֹצִיאוּ מִמִּצְרַיִם עֻגֹת מַצּוֹת כִּי לֹא חָמֵץ כִּי גֹרְשׁוּ מִמִּצְרַיִם וְלֹא יָכְלוּ לְהִתְמַהְמֵהַּ וְגַם צֵדָה לֹא עָשׂוּ לָהֶם:

Lift the *maror* and recite the following:

מָרוֹר זֶה שֶׁאָנוּ אוֹכְלִים עַל שׁוּם מָה. עַל שׁוּם שֶׁמֵּרְרוּ הַמִּצְרִים אֶת חַיֵּי אֲבוֹתֵינוּ בְּמִצְרָיִם. שֶׁנֶּאֱמַר וַיְמָרְרוּ אֶת חַיֵּיהֶם בַּעֲבֹדָה קָשָׁה בְּחֹמֶר וּבִלְבֵנִים וּבְכָל עֲבֹדָה בַּשָּׂדֶה אֵת כָּל עֲבֹדָתָם אֲשֶׁר עָבְדוּ בָהֶם בְּפָרֶךְ:

בְּכָל דּוֹר וָדוֹר חַיָּב אָדָם לִרְאוֹת אֶת עַצְמוֹ כְּאִלּוּ הוּא יָצָא מִמִּצְרַיִם. שֶׁנֶּאֱמַר וְהִגַּדְתָּ לְבִנְךָ בַּיּוֹם הַהוּא לֵאמֹר בַּעֲבוּר זֶה עָשָׂה יְיָ לִי בְּצֵאתִי מִמִּצְרָיִם. לֹא אֶת אֲבוֹתֵינוּ בִּלְבָד גָּאַל הַקָּדוֹשׁ בָּרוּךְ הוּא אֶלָּא אַף אוֹתָנוּ גָּאַל עִמָּהֶם. שֶׁנֶּאֱמַר וְאוֹתָנוּ הוֹצִיא מִשָּׁם לְמַעַן הָבִיא אוֹתָנוּ לָתֶת לָנוּ אֶת הָאָרֶץ אֲשֶׁר נִשְׁבַּע לַאֲבֹתֵינוּ:

difficulty of finding and marrying your soul mate is just like the difficulty of splitting the sea. You know why so many marriages break up? They don't love each other enough to change from water to dry land.

I want to bless you and me that we should always be ready to be anything for the people we love. For God I can be water, I can be fire, I can be dry land. For my child I would do anything in the world. The Talmud says that when we came to the Red Sea the children led the way. They're so open, so infinite; they want to be everything and they can be anything they want to be. The real redemption is on the seventh day, when we are so

Lift up the matzah and recite the following:

This matzah that we eat – what is its meaning? It is because our fathers' dough did not have time to rise before the King of kings, the Holy One, blessed is He, revealed Himself to them and redeemed them – as it says: "And they baked the dough which they had brought out of Egypt into cakes of matzah, for it had not leavened because they were driven out of Egypt and could not delay, nor had they prepared provisions for themselves."

Lift the maror and recite the following:

This bitter herb that we eat – what is its meaning? It is because the Egyptians embittered our fathers' lives in Egypt; as it says: "They embittered their lives with hard labor, with mortar and bricks, and with all manner of labor in the field: whatever work they made them do was with harshness."

In every generation it is one's duty to see himself as though he has personally gone out from Egypt, as it says: "You shall tell your son on that day: 'It was because of this [that we would serve Him in the future by refraining from chametz and eating matzah] that Hashem did [all these miracles] for me when I went out of Egypt.'" It was not only our fathers whom the Holy One redeemed from slavery; we too, were redeemed with them, as is written: "He brought us out from there in order to bring us to, and give us, the land which He promised to our fathers."

The matzos should be covered when the cup of wine is raised. Lift the cup of wine and say:

לְפִיכָךְ אֲנַחְנוּ חַיָּבִים לְהוֹדוֹת לְהַלֵּל לְשַׁבֵּחַ לְפָאֵר לְרוֹמֵם
לְהַדֵּר לְבָרֵךְ לְעַלֵּה וּלְקַלֵּס. לְמִי שֶׁעָשָׂה לַאֲבוֹתֵינוּ וְלָנוּ
אֶת כָּל הַנִּסִּים הָאֵלֶּה. הוֹצִיאָנוּ מֵעַבְדוּת לְחֵרוּת. מִיָּגוֹן
לְשִׂמְחָה. וּמֵאֵבֶל לְיוֹם טוֹב. וּמֵאֲפֵלָה לְאוֹר גָּדוֹל.
וּמִשִׁעְבּוּד לִגְאֻלָּה. וְנֹאמַר לְפָנָיו שִׁירָה חֲדָשָׁה הַלְלוּיָהּ.

redeemed, so free, that we could be anything in the world.

בעבור זה עשה ה' לי   Because of this Hashem did miracles

We have 613 mitzvos, 613 laws. I don't like the word "laws": it reminds me of the police, some straight character sitting there and telling us what to do. "Mitzvah" means something different; it means that Hashem gave us 613 ways to come close to Him. The ways are divided into two kinds, 248 ways of reaching God by doing certain things, and 365 ways of reaching Him by not doing certain things. When I have a chance to do something wrong, and I stop myself, something happens inside me. I walk a few steps higher.

לפיכך   Therefore

This story was told by the *heilige* Rebbe Asher Karliner. Somewhere in Russia there was a priest who preached in the church every Sunday. He preached a *gevalt*: inspiring, great sermons. The only problem was that he was always drunk. All the same, though, he preached really well.

Finally the people got together and told him, "If you're a drunkard, you must stop preaching." He said, "I'll try to stop drinking." But he couldn't, so then he said, "Let me give one last speech." And this is what he said: "It's true that I don't deserve to speak about God, but I can't help it. What can I do? I can't help preaching."

The matzos should be covered when the cup of wine is raised. Lift the cup of wine and say:

Therefore it is our duty to thank, praise, hail, glorify, exalt, honor, bless, extol and celebrate Him Who did all these miracles for our fathers and us. He brought us forth from slavery to freedom, from sorrow to joy, from mourning to festivity, from darkness to great light, and from servitude to redemption. Let us, therefore, say a new song before Him: Halleluyah!

מיגון לשמחה   **From sorrow to joy**

Rebbe Nachman says that the greatest sin in the world is to be sad, not to be filled with joy. My beautiful friends, all of us want so much, need so much. We don't have it, because of what happens when we ask for something from Heaven. Just think, when you ask for something from another human being, they're not going to pay attention to you unless you have a joyous heart. People are always happy to give to someone who's happy. So just imagine it: I'm asking for millions of tons from Heaven, and here the heavenly servant knocks on my door. He wants to give me everything I ordered; but when I open the door I'm sad, I'm broken-hearted. Who wants to have anything to do with a sad person? So they throw me a few crumbs and take off.

If you ask somebody for a favor and then you just sit there and cry, they can't get rid of you fast enough. But if you're filled with joy, if your heart is dancing and your eyes are shining, people want so much to be close to you.

People only hate when they're sad. If you're dreaming that one day the whole world will be one, you should know, it will only happen with joy.

Even deeper than that, God wants to give me so much that it needs a lot of strength to carry all of it. When you're full of joy you're full of strength, and you can carry anything — the whole world — on your shoulders.

We all have certain reflexes. They don't come from our head, they come from our insides. You don't like to shake hands with somebody that has dirty hands. Even if you have to because you have good manners, you don't want to, and you try to take your hand back as fast as possible. If someone has clean hands, you like to shake hands with him. If you love someone you can hold their hands forever. Our holy Rabbis teach us, sadness make us dirty. It's the spirit of uncleanness, unholiness, that descends upon us. Believe me, most friendships break up because there is not enough joy in them.

Rebbe Nachman says, "Why are you sad? Because everything goes wrong in your life. But *gevalt*, do you know why everything goes wrong? Because you're sad." If you ask me, "I'm so sad, how do I get happy?" — friends, believe me, I wish I knew the answer. I can only pray that God give you the gift of joy. Life is in God's hands, and He gives it to anyone He feels is fit for it. Even joy is in His hands, only it's your job to ask for it, and then He'll give it to you. Even if you're not fit, even for misfits like you and me, there's a way: to pray and pray. Every second you have to ask God, you have to cry and beg, "Let my heart be filled with joy."

Friends, one day there will be peace in the world, and suddenly God will give us as a gift the greatest joy in the world. You know, loneliness is such a deep sadness, and being one with another human being is such a great joy. Can you imagine being one with the whole world? What joy! Unbelievable!

When someone's sad he wants to run away from the world, from himself, from God. What happened to Adam and Eve? The first mistake: they ran away from God, from paradise. Sometimes you talk to your best friend, the person you love the most, but you can't get through to him. He's hiding, building walls around himself. But someone's a true friend if, when you tell him why you're sad, you're not sad any more. The holy Baal Shem Tov taught the world that every person needs a good friend.

Every child needs a father and mother. You know what parents are for? People think their biggest job is to tell the children when they're doing wrong. But that's not it; parents are someone for the children to run to.

Chavah knew from the moment of her creation that she was in this world to bring forth children. She thought to herself, "What's the greatest thing I can do for my children? I'll eat from the Tree of Knowledge and I'll tell them what's right and what's wrong." God said to her, "Look at yourself: you're hiding in the garden, you're running away from Me. Don't you know what a mother is for? When the children are crying, they run to their mother or their father." So Hashem said to Chavah, "I'm sorry, it's going to be hard for you to have children, because you don't know the secret of what parents are really for."

So you hear me, brothers and sisters, fathers and mothers, all over the world, I bless you: When your children are crying, may they come running to you. I bless myself, all of us, that instead of running away from each other, together we'll run to the One, to the Only One, Who brought us out from sorrow to joy.

ונאמר לפניו שירה חדשה   Say a new song before Him

I would like to pour out my heart to you. The Torah tells us that when our father Avraham met Shem, who was the High Priest then, he brought out wine and bread in his honor. Our holy Rabbis teach us that the older wine gets the better it tastes; but bread is only good when it is fresh. The world needs bread: the world has such longing for new revelations, for new teaching, for new lights, for new ideas, for everything new. Yet in the deepest depths it's crying for the old wine.

Shem the high priest saw Abraham, God's spokesman to the world until today. Where would we be without our father Avraham? This is what Shem told him: "Avraham, if you want to be closer to people and to bring people closer to God, you have to know the secret of bread and wine. You have to know that when a person comes and is crying for bread, you must give him fresh bread. God gives us new things all the time. We say in our prayers *hamechadesh betuvo,* that God renews the Creation every day. The truth is that God renews the whole world every second; God is never old, and the Torah is never old. Sometimes, Avraham, you have to know that people come crying for old wine. Always have a drop of wine for them."

But the deepest truth is that God's word — anything which is holy, precious, and beautiful — is always new and old together. I knew everything beautiful yesterday, and today I'm seeing it all for the first time. I've known my children since the moment they were born, but each time I see them it's like the first time.

I want to share something with you, sweetest friends: You know when you kiss your wife whom you love very much, you close your eyes and you open them. You're saying, "I've known you for eternity, but I'm seeing you now for the first time."

My dear friends, I feel that there was never a generation which had such a craving for something new. We're living in a world where so many old ideas have gone bankrupt. We look at the lives of so many people whom we exalted, people we thought were great. Now we realize they were actually bankrupt, so we look for something new. But in the deepest depths we want the old wine. We want God to reveal to us every word he taught our forefathers on Mount Sinai and in Yerushalayim, our holy city.

This summer I had the privilege, the sad privilege, to play for wounded soldiers. At one concert I played for soldiers who were wounded in their eyes. There was a soldier who could barely see at all. I walked in there, and suddenly he said to someone, "Please help me on to the table. I want to dance." Out of nowhere a melody came to my heart and my soul. Very seldom does a melody come to me together with the words, but at that

הַלְלוּיָהּ הַלְלוּ עַבְדֵי יְיָ הַלְלוּ אֶת שֵׁם יְיָ. יְהִי שֵׁם יְיָ מְבֹרָךְ מֵעַתָּה וְעַד עוֹלָם. מִמִּזְרַח שֶׁמֶשׁ עַד מְבוֹאוֹ מְהֻלָּל שֵׁם יְיָ. רָם עַל כָּל גּוֹיִם יְיָ עַל הַשָּׁמַיִם כְּבוֹדוֹ. מִי כַּיְיָ אֱלֹהֵינוּ הַמַּגְבִּיהִי לָשָׁבֶת. הַמַּשְׁפִּילִי לִרְאוֹת בַּשָּׁמַיִם וּבָאָרֶץ. מְקִימִי מֵעָפָר דָּל מֵאַשְׁפֹּת יָרִים אֶבְיוֹן. לְהוֹשִׁיבִי עִם נְדִיבִים עִם נְדִיבֵי עַמּוֹ. מוֹשִׁיבִי עֲקֶרֶת הַבַּיִת אֵם הַבָּנִים שְׂמֵחָה הַלְלוּיָהּ:

בְּצֵאת יִשְׂרָאֵל מִמִּצְרַיִם בֵּית יַעֲקֹב מֵעַם לֹעֵז. הָיְתָה יְהוּדָה לְקָדְשׁוֹ יִשְׂרָאֵל מַמְשְׁלוֹתָיו. הַיָּם רָאָה וַיָּנֹס הַיַּרְדֵּן יִסֹּב לְאָחוֹר. הֶהָרִים רָקְדוּ כְאֵילִים גְּבָעוֹת כִּבְנֵי צֹאן. מַה לְּךָ הַיָּם כִּי תָנוּס הַיַּרְדֵּן תִּסֹּב לְאָחוֹר. הֶהָרִים תִּרְקְדוּ כְאֵילִים גְּבָעוֹת כִּבְנֵי צֹאן. מִלִּפְנֵי אָדוֹן חוּלִי אָרֶץ מִלִּפְנֵי אֱלוֹהַּ יַעֲקֹב. הַהֹפְכִי הַצּוּר אֲגַם מָיִם חַלָּמִישׁ לְמַעְיְנוֹ מָיִם:

moment the words came right along with it.

We say *v'sham nashir shir chadash*, that when the Holy Temple is rebuilt our hearts will be filled again and we'll sing a new song — the old song will be renewed. Friends, I want you to know that this holy soldier danced on the table for a whole hour. He couldn't stop dancing and we couldn't stop singing. So here's my prayer for all the wounded soldiers, all the people in pain, all the people who are still blind, still waiting for God to give them new eyes. May God give them a taste of the new song that we'll someday sing.

הֶהָרִים רָקְדוּ   **The mountains skipped**

A long time ago we lived on the hills of Yerushalayim, but then we went

Halleluyah! Praise His mighty deeds, you servants of Hashem, praise the Name of Hashem. Blessed be the Name of Hashem from now and forever. From the rising of the sun to its setting, praised be the name of Hashem. Supreme above all nations is Hashem, above the heavens is His glory. Who is like Hashem, our God, Who is enthroned on high, yet looks down upon the heaven and earth? He raises the poor from the dust, from the trash heaps He lifts the pauper – to seat them with nobles, with the nobles of His people. He transforms a childless woman into a joyous mother of children: Halleluyah! When Israel went out from Egypt, the house of Yaakov from a people of a different tongue, Yehudah became His sanctuary, Israel His dominion. The sea saw and fled; the Jordan turned backward. The mountains skipped like rams, and the hills like young lambs. "What ails you, sea, that you flee, Jordan, that you turn backward? Mountains, that you skip like rams, hills, like young lambs?" Before the Lord's presence tremble, earth, before the God of Yaakov, Who turns the rock into a pond of water, the flint into a flowing fountain.

into exile. We went into the valley. One valley was called the Inquisition, one was called Auschwitz, and the last valley was called Siberia. How can the hill dance, as long as the valley is still in exile? But the great day will

If the cup has been put down in the meantime, raise it again for the following blessing:

בָּרוּךְ אַתָּה יְיָ אֱלֹהֵינוּ מֶלֶךְ הָעוֹלָם אֲשֶׁר גְּאָלָנוּ וְגָאַל אֶת אֲבוֹתֵינוּ מִמִּצְרַיִם. וְהִגִּיעָנוּ הַלַּיְלָה הַזֶּה לֶאֱכָל בּוֹ מַצָּה וּמָרוֹר. כֵּן יְיָ אֱלֹהֵינוּ וֵאלֹהֵי אֲבוֹתֵינוּ יַגִּיעֵנוּ לְמוֹעֲדִים וְלִרְגָלִים אֲחֵרִים הַבָּאִים לִקְרָאתֵנוּ לְשָׁלוֹם שְׂמֵחִים בְּבִנְיַן עִירֶךָ וְשָׂשִׂים בַּעֲבוֹדָתֶךָ. וְנֹאכַל שָׁם מִן הַזְּבָחִים וּמִן הַפְּסָחִים (בְּמוֹצָ"ש"ק אוֹמְרִים מִן הַפְּסָחִים וּמִן הַזְּבָחִים) אֲשֶׁר יַגִּיעַ דָּמָם עַל קִיר מִזְבַּחֲךָ לְרָצוֹן וְנוֹדֶה לְךָ שִׁיר חָדָשׁ עַל גְּאֻלָּתֵנוּ וְעַל פְּדוּת נַפְשֵׁנוּ: בָּרוּךְ אַתָּה יְיָ גָּאַל יִשְׂרָאֵל:

בָּרוּךְ אַתָּה יְיָ אֱלֹהֵינוּ מֶלֶךְ הָעוֹלָם בּוֹרֵא פְּרִי הַגָּפֶן

The second cup is drunk while leaning on the left side.

come when from all the four corners of the world, from all the valleys, we will come back to Yerushalayim. The valley people will tell the hill people, "When you were crying your tears rolled into the valley; and your tears come from so high." The hill people will tell the valley people, "Your prayers rose up to the hills; and your prayers come from so deep." Then the valleys and the hills will come together. The six million will dance together with the three million from Russia. Israel and the world will sing together, God will sing with the angels, we will sing with God. Yerushalayim and the whole world will dance together on the holy hills.

ונודה לך שיר חדש   We will thank You with a new song

My beautiful friends, we're still singing old melodies. Everything is old, *Yiddishkeit* is old — not real *Yiddishkeit*, but *Yiddishkeit* the way we're doing it and teaching it. Shabbos is old. Whatever we think of Yerushalayim, or of each other, is old. My deepest prayer in the name of all of us is *v'sham nashir shir chadash*, Master of the world, put a new song into our hearts!

You know, my friends, I've walked the streets of Yerushalayim, Tel Aviv,

If the cup has been put down in the meantime, raise it again for the following blessing:

Blessed are You, Hashem, our God, King of the universe, Who redeemed us and our fathers from Egypt and enabled us to reach this night that we may eat matzah and maror on it. So may Hashem, our God and God of our fathers, enable us to reach future festivals and holidays in peace, rejoicing in the rebuilding of Your city and ecstatic in Your service. And there we will eat of the offerings and Pesach sacrifices whose blood will reach the sides of Your altar for gracious acceptance. We will then thank You with a new song for our redemption and for the liberation of our souls. Blessed are You, Hashem, Who has redeemed Israel.

Blessed are You, Hashem, our God, King of the universe, Creator of the fruit of the vine.

The second cup is drunk while leaning on the left side.

Haifa, Beer Sheva. I look at the young people, and you know what they need? A *shir chadash*, a new song to sing. I walk in the streets of New York, of Paris, of Rome, of Stockholm, and I see the eyes of the people. You know what they're crying for? A *shir chadash*.

A new song comes only from the Holy City — *v'sham nashir*, from there we'll sing. One day the whole world will learn from us to sing a new song: a song without hatred, a song with just love.

רחצה

All now wash their hands and say the blessing. It is the custom to bring water and a basin to the leader of the Seder at the table, as a symbol of the royal status that prevails on Seder night.

בָּרוּךְ אַתָּה יְיָ אֱלֹהֵינוּ מֶלֶךְ הָעוֹלָם אֲשֶׁר קִדְּשָׁנוּ בְּמִצְוֹתָיו
וְצִוָּנוּ עַל נְטִילַת יָדָיִם:

מוציא

The leader of the Seder picks up the matzos and says the following blessings. All should concentrate on fulfilling the commandment of eating matzah, and be sure to eat the proper amount (it is best to take two *kazeísim*) within the correct amount of time (about four minutes). The matzah is eaten while leaning on the left side.

בָּרוּךְ אַתָּה יְיָ אֱלֹהֵינוּ מֶלֶךְ הָעוֹלָם הַמּוֹצִיא לֶחֶם מִן הָאָרֶץ:

מצה

בָּרוּךְ אַתָּה יְיָ אֱלֹהֵינוּ מֶלֶךְ הָעוֹלָם אֲשֶׁר קִדְּשָׁנוּ בְּמִצְוֹתָיו
וְצִוָּנוּ עַל אֲכִילַת מַצָּה:

מוציא מצה   **Motzi Matzah**

My father was appointed to the Rabbinate of Berlin a little before Purim, at the end of the First World War. A few days after Purim he received a letter from a soldier serving at the front. (Most of the soldiers sent to the front never returned.) The letter said, "My name is Moishele Cohen. I'm the only matzah baker in my whole home town. If I don't come home immediately there won't be any matzos in my town for Pesach, so please go to General So-and-so and beg him to give me some leave so I can come home and bake matzah."

Rochtzah

All now wash their hands and say the blessing. It is the custom to bring water and a basin
to the leader of the Seder at the table, as a symbol of the royal status that prevails on Seder
night.

Blessed are You, Hashem, our God, King of the
universe, Who has sanctified us with His commandments, and has commanded us to observe the wash-
ing of the hands.

Motzi

The leader of the Seder picks up the matzos and says the following blessings. All should
concentrate on fulfilling the commandment of eating matzah, and be sure to eat the proper
amount (it is best to take two *kazeísim*) within the correct amount of time (about four
minutes). The matzah is eaten while leaning on the left side.

Blessed are You, Hashem, our God, King of the
universe, Who brings forth bread from the earth.

Matzah

Blessed are You, Hashem, our God, King of the
universe, Who has sanctified us with His commandments, and has commanded us to observe the eating
of matzah.

You only had to show this letter to anyone, and if he had a brain in his
head he'd tell you not to waste your time. To try and get leave for this
soldier was a big joke. It was the desperate end of the war. Every day
thousands of soldiers were dying, and there was nothing to eat in Berlin; and
you think the General Staff had nothing on their minds besides matzos? My

father, yes, he was an important Rabbi with a big *shul*, but to come to the General in the middle of a war and tell him we need matzos! For us it's life-and-death, but what would it be to him? Crazy.

But my father had a pure soul. He said, "I didn't ask for this letter, the letter came to me. I must go."

Dearest friends, in my life I never saw my father without a *sefer* in his hands. This time too, he took with him a few *sefarim*, because who knew how much time he'd have to wait to speak to the General? When he got there he saw hundreds of people waiting. The General had several officers who did nothing but take down names and give out numbers — my father understood that it would be days until he got to speak to the General. What did he do? He gave in his name and continued learning.

A few minutes later an officer came over to my father and said, "Rabbi, the General asks you to come to him immediately. He must see you."

He walked in to the General's office, and the General took my father's hand and kissed it. Unbelievable! What is going on? He asked, "Aren't you the son of Rabbi Shlomo Carlebach, the Rabbi of Lübeck?" My father said, "Yes, I'm his youngest son." He said to my father, "Whatever you want will be done." My father said right away, "I need to bring a soldier from the French front back to his home town." He said, "Just give me his ID number." And right away he dispatched an order to the staff in France to send Moishe le Cohen home.

My father asked the General, "How do you know my father?" — But if I want you to understand how that happened, I have to take a minute and tell you another story first.

In the early nineteen hundreds, thousands and thousands of Jewish youths from Germany left for America. To our sorrow, their parents lost all connection with them. This left thousands of parents without any help or support when they grew old. There were old people simply dying in their houses without anyone even realizing. My grandfather, the Rabbi of Lübeck, thought, "I must build an old age home for these people." He decided he would look for new contributors, people that never gave to holy causes like this before. He heard that the banker of the German Kaiser was a Jew. Why was he a Jew? Simply because the Kaiser never asked him to convert — all the Kaiser worried about was that he should take care of the money. But if the Kaiser asked him to convert, he would; that's what they told my grandfather about him. This man had certainly never associated himself with anything Jewish. But what do we know about a Jewish soul, the depths of the Jewish soul?

My grandfather went to Baron von Bleichroeder's palace, and they brought him to his office. All of a sudden the Baron stood up when he saw my grandfather. He went over to him, kissed his hand, and started crying. He said, "Rabbi, you must know that God sent you to me. I'm seventy years old; today is my birthday, and last night I cried the whole night. I thought, 'I'm Jewish, but I've never spoken to my brethren. I never spoke to someone who could purify my soul.' Today you came to me."

They became close friends. Anything that my grandfather asked of him, the Baron did immediately. He built a huge building for an old age home. It was the first old age home in Germany, and probably the first in the whole of Europe. (To our great sorrow the building was totally destroyed, because the Nazis, *yimach shmam,* made it into their headquarters.) After five years during which my grandfather spoke with the Baron almost every day, he got a call from the Baron's son, who said, "Holy Rabbi, you were my father's best friend. My father wasn't a simple man. This morning I entered his office and saw a letter on his desk. This is what was written: 'If, God forbid, I don't get up tomorrow morning, I want only Rabbi Carlebach to eulogize me. If he cannot, I don't want any eulogy.' I ran into my father's bedroom, but he was already in Heaven."

My grandfather said a *hesped,* a eulogy for the Baron, and understandably, the Kaiser of Germany with all his family came to the funeral. The brother of the Czar of Russia came too, and the kings of England, Denmark, Sweden, Norway — all the European leaders.

Now I can return to the original story with the General. When my father asked him how he knew the Rabbi of Lübeck, he answered, "I was fortunate enough to be there when Rabbi Carlebach eulogized Baron von Bleichroeder. Let me tell you, generals don't cry and they don't laugh. My heart is dead, and my soul died before I was born, because you can't be a general and remain a person. I don't believe in anything; if you came and told me that half the world just died, I wouldn't blink an eye. But one time in my life I cried like a baby for a quarter of an hour. Once in my life I believed in people, in a living God. Once in my life I prayed that God would forgive my sins. That was when your father spoke."

מָרוֹר

The leader of the Seder takes a *kazayis* of *maror*, dips it into *charoses* and then shakes off the *charoses*. Then he gives the same amount to all that are present. The following blessing is recited, with the intention that it also applies to the *maror* eaten during Korech. The *maror* is eaten without reclining, and must be eaten within the proper amount of time. All should concentrate on fulfilling the commandment of eating *maror* on Pesach night.

בָּרוּךְ אַתָּה יְיָ אֱלֹהֵינוּ מֶלֶךְ הָעוֹלָם אֲשֶׁר קִדְּשָׁנוּ בְּמִצְוֹתָיו וְצִוָּנוּ עַל אֲכִילַת מָרוֹר:

כּוֹרֵךְ

The bottom matzah is now taken. From it everyone at the Seder receives a *kazayis* (other matzos may be used as a supplement if there is not enough for everyone), together with a *kazayis* of *maror* (dipped into *charoses*, which is shaken off). The "sandwich" is eaten while reclining. Before eating it, say this:

זֵכֶר לְמִקְדָּשׁ כְּהִלֵּל. כֵּן עָשָׂה הִלֵּל בִּזְמַן שֶׁבֵּית הַמִּקְדָּשׁ הָיָה קַיָּם הָיָה כּוֹרֵךְ מַצָּה וּמָרוֹר וְאוֹכֵל בְּיַחַד לְקַיֵּם מַה שֶׁנֶּאֱמַר עַל מַצּוֹת וּמְרוֹרִים יֹאכְלֻהוּ:

שֻׁלְחָן עוֹרֵךְ

It is a custom to eat a hard-boiled egg at the beginning of the meal. No roasted meat should be eaten, for this might be mistaken for the Pesach sacrifice, which it is forbidden to offer in Exile. One should try to recline throughout the meal.

שׁוּלְחָן עוֹרֵךְ   **Shulchan Orech**

In the time of the Yeshuos Yaakov there was a *Yid* in Lemberg who was so hungry you couldn't even call it fasting. "Fasting" means that sometimes you eat and sometimes you don't. But he never ate. *Nebach*, once a year he got to eat: the Yeshuos Yaakov got the community together on Pesach every year to give food, so this man and his family would have something to eat.

One year, in the middle of the Seder this poor *Yiddele* came running to the Yeshuos Yaakov. They didn't have caterers back then; they would take

Maror

The leader of the Seder takes a *kazayis* of *maror*, dips it into *charoses* and then shakes off the *charoses*. Then he gives the same amount to all that are present. The following blessing is recited, with the intention that it also applies to the *maror* eaten during Korech. The *maror* is eaten without reclining, and must be eaten within the proper amount of time. All should concentrate on fulfilling the commandment of eating *maror* on Pesach night.

Blessed are You, Hashem, our God, King of the universe, Who has sanctified us with His commandments, and has commanded us to observe the eating of maror.

Korech

The bottom matzah is now taken. From it everyone at the Seder receives a *kazayis* (other matzos may be used as a supplement if there is not enough for everyone), together with a *kazayis* of *maror* (dipped into *charoses*, which is shaken off). The "sandwich" is eaten while reclining. Before eating it, say this:

In remembrance of the Temple, we do as Hillel did at the time when the Temple was standing. He would combine matzah and maror in a sandwich and eat them together, to fulfill what is written in the Torah, "with matzos and bitter herbs shall they eat it."

Shulchan Orech

It is a custom to eat a hard-boiled egg at the beginning of the meal. No roasted meat should be eaten, for this might be mistaken for the Pesach sacrifice, which it is forbidden to offer in Exile. One should try to recline throughout the meal.

one big pot, throw everything in, and cook it. One of the poor man's children just threw something into the pot, and he was pretty sure it was *chametz*.

Everybody knows that with *chametz* even *b'elef*, even if it's only one part in a thousand, there's no way out. The whole pot is *chametz*. Okay now,

צפון

After the meal everyone must eat a *kazayis* of the *Afikoman* while reclining. Some say that one must eat a *kabeitzah*. It is best to eat the *Afikoman* by midnight. If the Seder is running late, the following condition can be made: Eat a *kazayis* of matzah right away, and have in mind that if the last time to eat is midnight, this is the *Afikoman*. Then wait till after midnight, and then proceed with the regular order of the Seder. After the *Afikoman* is eaten, one should refrain from eating and drinking, except for the last two cups of wine.

ברך

שִׁיר הַמַּעֲלוֹת בְּשׁוּב יְיָ אֶת שִׁיבַת צִיּוֹן הָיִינוּ כְּחֹלְמִים:
אָז יִמָּלֵא שְׂחוֹק פִּינוּ וּלְשׁוֹנֵנוּ רִנָּה אָז יֹאמְרוּ בַגּוֹיִם
הִגְדִּיל יְיָ לַעֲשׂוֹת עִם אֵלֶּה: הִגְדִּיל יְיָ לַעֲשׂוֹת עִמָּנוּ
הָיִינוּ שְׂמֵחִים: שׁוּבָה יְיָ אֶת שְׁבִיתֵנוּ כַּאֲפִיקִים בַּנֶּגֶב:
הַזֹּרְעִים בְּדִמְעָה בְּרִנָּה יִקְצֹרוּ: הָלוֹךְ יֵלֵךְ וּבָכֹה נֹשֵׂא
מֶשֶׁךְ הַזָּרַע בֹּא יָבֹא בְרִנָּה נֹשֵׂא אֲלֻמֹּתָיו:

open your hearts. There's one opinion, the *heilige* Rav Achai Gaon, that although *chametz* isn't *batel b'shishim* it is *batel b'meiah*. With other *treifeh* things, if there's sixty parts of other stuff in the pot it's all kosher; and Rav Achai Gaon says, although that's not true with *chametz* if there are a hundred other parts it's all right.

We don't hold this way, because only Rav Achai says it, but now the Yeshuos Yaakov is thinking, "It's Seder night. *Gevalt*, if the pot is *chametz* he'll have nothing to eat, and he has eleven children." He thinks, "Reb Achai Gaon can carry this; he has broad shoulders." He says to the *Yid*, "Go home; it's a hundred percent kosher." That night Rav Achai came to the Yeshuos Yaakov in a dream and said, "Thank you so much, because, I want you to know, I only wrote that decision of mine for the sake of this one *Yid.*"

It's awesome. A thousand years beforehand, Rav Achai saw with the *ruach hakodesh*, with holy foresight he saw one *Yid* in Lemberg. Now you know what kind of sages we've had. So whenever I say *Amar Abayei*, that Abayei said this or that, it has to be clear to me that when he said it he was thinking of me. When the Torah's being left uncared for in a dark alley, it

Tzafun

After the meal everyone must eat a *kazayis* of the *Afikoman* while reclining. Some say that one must eat a *kabeitzah*. It is best to eat the *Afikoman* by midnight. If the Seder is running late, the following condition can be made: Eat a *kazayis* of matzah right away, and have in mind that if the last time to eat is midnight, this is the *Afikoman*. Then wait till after midnight, and then proceed with the regular order of the Seder. After the *Afikoman* is eaten, one should refrain from eating and drinking, except for the last two cups of wine.

Barech

A song of ascents. When Hashem returns the captivity of Zion we are like dreamers. Then our mouth will be filled with laughter and our tongue with singing. Then they will say among the nations, "Hashem has done great things with these." Hashem has done great things with us; we were happy. Return our captivity, Hashem, like water-springs in the southern desert. Those who sow with tears will reap with great joy. Though he goes on his way weeping as he carries the seeds through the field, he will return singing, bearing his sheaves.

---

has to be clear to us that Rashi, Tosafos, R. Akiva Eiger, they were all thinking of us. Today, even if our heads aren't as great as earlier generations, we have such *siyata dishmaya*. Heaven helps us to understand the Torah.

שיר המעלות   **A song of ascents**

Hazor'im b'dim'ah, if you work with tears, if whatever you do is with

If three adult males are present, say the following invitation:

הַמְזַמֵּן אוֹמֵר: רַבּוֹתַי נְבָרֵךְ (מִיר װֶעלְן בֶּענְטְשִׁין)

הַמְסוּבִּין: יְהִי שֵׁם יְיָ מְבוֹרָךְ מֵעַתָּה וְעַד עוֹלָם

If ten men are present the words in brackets are added.

הַמְזַמֵּן: יְהִי שֵׁם יְיָ מְבוֹרָךְ מֵעַתָּה וְעַד עוֹלָם. בִּרְשׁוּת מָרָנָן וְרַבָּנָן וְרַבּוֹתַי נְבָרֵךְ (בעשרה אֱלֹהֵינוּ) שֶׁאָכַלְנוּ מִשֶּׁלּוֹ.

הַמְסוּבִּין: בָּרוּךְ (בעשרה אֱלֹהֵינוּ) שֶׁאָכַלְנוּ מִשֶּׁלּוֹ וּבְטוּבוֹ חָיִינוּ.

The leader repeats the above and then says:

יָחִיד אֵינוּ אוֹמֵר: בָּרוּךְ הוּא וּבָרוּךְ שְׁמוֹ

בָּרוּךְ אַתָּה יְיָ אֱלֹהֵינוּ מֶלֶךְ הָעוֹלָם הַזָּן אֶת הָעוֹלָם כֻּלּוֹ בְּטוּבוֹ בְּחֵן בְּחֶסֶד וּבְרַחֲמִים הוּא נוֹתֵן לֶחֶם לְכָל בָּשָׂר כִּי לְעוֹלָם חַסְדּוֹ. וּבְטוּבוֹ הַגָּדוֹל תָּמִיד לֹא חָסַר לָנוּ וְאַל יֶחְסַר לָנוּ מָזוֹן לְעוֹלָם וָעֶד. בַּעֲבוּר שְׁמוֹ הַגָּדוֹל כִּי הוּא אֵל זָן וּמְפַרְנֵס לַכֹּל וּמֵטִיב לַכֹּל וּמֵכִין מָזוֹן לְכָל בְּרִיּוֹתָיו אֲשֶׁר בָּרָא. בָּרוּךְ אַתָּה יְיָ הַזָּן אֶת הַכֹּל:

tears, then *b'rinah yiktzoru*, you'll reap with joy. That's what the words mean; but old Chassidim, old *Yidden* who knew the truth, knew that these words hold the secret of being real. They mean *hazor'im b'dim'ah b'rinah*, whatever you do it's with tears and joy together. You do everything with joy and with tears together. Whatever we do, whether planting or reaping, it's going to be with both joy and tears, for in this world nothing can ever be composed of only one of them.

If three adult males are present, say the following invitation:

(Leader:) Gentlemen, let us say Grace.

(Others:) Blessed be the name of Hashem from this time and forever!

If ten men are present the words in brackets are added.

(Leader:) Blessed be the name of Hashem from this time and forever! With your permission, let us bless [our God], from Whose abundance we have eaten.

(Others:) Blessed is [our God], from Whose abundance we have eaten and through Whose goodness we live.

The leader repeats the above and then says:

Blessed is He and blessed is His Name.

Blessed are You, Hashem, our God, King of the universe, Who nourishes the whole world with His goodness, with grace, with kindness, and with compassion. He gives nourishment to all flesh, for His kindness is forever. And through His great goodness we have never lacked, and may we never lack food forever – for the sake of His great Name, for it is He, God, Who provides and sustains all, and does good to all, and He prepares food for all of His creatures which He has created. Blessed are you, Hashem, Who provides for all.

נוֹדֶה לְךָ יְיָ אֱלֹהֵינוּ עַל שֶׁהִנְחַלְתָּ לַאֲבוֹתֵינוּ אֶרֶץ חֶמְדָּה
טוֹבָה וּרְחָבָה וְעַל שֶׁהוֹצֵאתָנוּ יְיָ אֱלֹהֵינוּ מֵאֶרֶץ מִצְרַיִם
וּפְדִיתָנוּ מִבֵּית עֲבָדִים וְעַל בְּרִיתְךָ שֶׁחָתַמְתָּ בִּבְשָׂרֵנוּ וְעַל
תּוֹרָתְךָ שֶׁלִּמַּדְתָּנוּ וְעַל חֻקֶּיךָ שֶׁהוֹדַעְתָּנוּ וְעַל חַיִּים חֵן
וָחֶסֶד שֶׁחוֹנַנְתָּנוּ וְעַל אֲכִילַת מָזוֹן שָׁאַתָּה זָן וּמְפַרְנֵס אוֹתָנוּ
תָּמִיד בְּכָל יוֹם וּבְכָל עֵת וּבְכָל שָׁעָה:

וְעַל הַכֹּל יְיָ אֱלֹהֵינוּ אֲנַחְנוּ מוֹדִים לָךְ וּמְבָרְכִים אוֹתָךְ יִתְבָּרַךְ
שִׁמְךָ בְּפִי כָּל חַי תָּמִיד לְעוֹלָם וָעֶד כַּכָּתוּב וְאָכַלְתָּ וְשָׂבָעְתָּ
וּבֵרַכְתָּ אֶת יְיָ אֱלֹהֶיךָ עַל הָאָרֶץ הַטּוֹבָה אֲשֶׁר נָתַן לָךְ.
בָּרוּךְ אַתָּה יְיָ עַל הָאָרֶץ וְעַל הַמָּזוֹן:

For Your Torah   עַל תּוֹרָתְךָ שֶׁלִּמַּדְתָּנוּ

You know, my beautiful friends, we all feel that Pesach is so special, but each one of us feels it in his own way. Every *Yid* is looking for his own words, to describe what he feels is so special about Pesach. Let me tell you about my own feelings.

We have this holiday of Pesach, when we celebrate how Hashem took us out of Egypt. Then comes the holiday of Shavuos, that celebrates the fact that God gave us the Torah. There is a difference between these two holidays — there are a lot of differences, but in a nutshell, on Shavuos you don't have to sit up with your children until late at night. It's beautiful if you do, but there's no special commandment that tells you to sit and tell them, "Tomorrow God is going to give us the Torah." On Pesach, though, there is such a mitzvah. On Pesach I have to sit with my children, even all night long, and tell them about the Exodus. *Gevalt,* the night is so deep — I'm sitting with them until the coming of *Mashiach.* I'm telling them about the One God Who took us out of Egypt, and Who chose us to be His people, and uplifted us, and made us special by giving us the Torah.

The Torah was only put here, in this world, for the Jewish Nation to use. How do you use the Torah? You learn from it to become holy, to become

We thank You, Hashem, our God, because You have given to our fathers as a heritage a desirable, good and spacious land; and because You brought us out, Hashem our God, from the land of Egypt, and You redeemed us from the house of slavery; and for Your covenant which You have sealed in our flesh; and for Your Torah which You have taught us and for Your laws which You have granted us; and for the food which You provide for us and sustain us with constantly, in every day, in every season, and in every hour.

For all this, Hashem our God, we thank You and bless You. May Your Name be blessed by the mouth of all the living, continuously and forever, as it is written: "When you have eaten and you are satisfied, you shall bless Hashem, your God, for the good land which He gave you." Blessed are You, Hashem, for the Land and for food.

God's own nation. But that's not something that just anyone can teach you. From a teacher you can learn every word of the Torah, but who can put the feeling of holiness in your heart, the feeling that the Torah was given to us by God, that we and God are the highest oneness in the world? That's something only parents can do.

And that's why we have the special mitzvah to teach our children on Seder night. Because on Pesach God gives us a taste of what it is to be a *Yid*, and only your parents can really get that across to you. What a privilege, to be able to put this feeling in a child's heart! What a gift! I tell my child, "When we made you there were three partners: your father, your mother, and God. Tonight I can tell you about the third partner."

רַחֵם נָא יְיָ אֱלֹהֵינוּ עַל יִשְׂרָאֵל עַמֶּךָ וְעַל יְרוּשָׁלַיִם עִירֶךָ וְעַל צִיּוֹן מִשְׁכַּן כְּבוֹדֶךָ וְעַל מַלְכוּת בֵּית דָּוִד מְשִׁיחֶךָ וְעַל הַבַּיִת הַגָּדוֹל וְהַקָּדוֹשׁ שֶׁנִּקְרָא שִׁמְךָ עָלָיו אֱלֹהֵינוּ אָבִינוּ רְעֵנוּ זוּנֵנוּ פַּרְנְסֵנוּ וְכַלְכְּלֵנוּ וְהַרְוִיחֵנוּ וְהַרְוַח לָנוּ יְיָ אֱלֹהֵינוּ מְהֵרָה מִכָּל צָרוֹתֵינוּ וְנָא עַל תַּצְרִיכֵנוּ יְיָ אֱלֹהֵינוּ לֹא לִידֵי מַתְּנַת בָּשָׂר וָדָם וְלֹא לִידֵי הַלְוָאָתָם כִּי אִם לְיָדְךָ הַמְּלֵאָה הַפְּתוּחָה הַקְּדוֹשָׁה וְהָרְחָבָה שֶׁלֹּא נֵבוֹשׁ וְלֹא נִכָּלֵם לְעוֹלָם וָעֶד:

The following paragraph is included on Shabbos:

רְצֵה וְהַחֲלִיצֵנוּ יְיָ אֱלֹהֵינוּ בְּמִצְוֹתֶיךָ וּבְמִצְוַת יוֹם הַשְּׁבִיעִי הַשַּׁבָּת הַגָּדוֹל וְהַקָּדוֹשׁ הַזֶּה כִּי יוֹם זֶה גָּדוֹל וְקָדוֹשׁ הוּא לְפָנֶיךָ לִשְׁבָּת בּוֹ וְלָנוּחַ בּוֹ בְּאַהֲבָה כְּמִצְוַת רְצוֹנֶךָ וּבִרְצוֹנְךָ הָנִיחַ לָנוּ יְיָ אֱלֹהֵינוּ שֶׁלֹּא תְהֵא צָרָה וְיָגוֹן וַאֲנָחָה בְּיוֹם מְנוּחָתֵנוּ וְהַרְאֵנוּ יְיָ אֱלֹהֵינוּ בְּנֶחָמַת צִיּוֹן עִירֶךָ וּבְבִנְיַן יְרוּשָׁלַיִם עִיר קָדְשֶׁךָ כִּי אַתָּה הוּא בַּעַל הַיְשׁוּעוֹת וּבַעַל הַנֶּחָמוֹת:

On the great and holy House
ועל הבית

When the Holy Temple is rebuilt, the prophet says it will be *"beis tefillah l'khol ha'amim,* My house will be called a house of prayer for all the nations of the world." Someday the world will realize there's no other way. "Wars don't bring us anywhere," they'll say. "Hatred doesn't lead us anywhere. There's only one way, we know that now. Let's all run to Yerushalayim, the holy city, to the One and Only One." And at that moment the whole world will run to God and to each other, and everything will be filled with joy.

Have mercy, Hashem, our God, on Israel Your people; on Yerushalayim, Your city; on Zion, the resting place of Your Glory; on the kingdom of the house of David, Your anointed; and on the great and holy House upon which Your Name is called. Our God, our Father, tend us, provide for us, sustain us, support us, relieve us; grant us, Hashem our God, relief from all our troubles. Please do not make us, Hashem our God, needful of the gifts of humans or their loans, but only needful of Your full, open, holy, and generous Hand, that we be not shamed or humiliated for ever and ever.

The following paragraph is included on Shabbos:

May you be pleased to give us rest, Hashem our God, through Your commandments and through the commandment of the seventh day, this great and holy Shabbos. For this day is great and holy before You, to refrain from work on it and to rest on it with love, in accordance with Your will. May it be Your will to grant us rest, Hashem our God, that there be no distress, grief, or moaning on this day of our rest. And show us, Hashem our God, the consolation of Zion, Your city, and the rebuilding of Yerushalayim, Your holy city, for You are the Master of salvations and Master of consolations.

אֱלֹהֵינוּ וֵאלֹהֵי אֲבוֹתֵינוּ יַעֲלֶה וְיָבֹא וְיַגִּיעַ וְיֵרָאֶה וְיֵרָצֶה
וְיִשָּׁמַע וְיִפָּקֵד וְיִזָּכֵר זִכְרוֹנֵנוּ וּפִקְדוֹנֵנוּ וְזִכְרוֹן אֲבוֹתֵינוּ וְזִכְרוֹן
מָשִׁיחַ בֶּן דָּוִד עַבְדֶּךָ וְזִכְרוֹן יְרוּשָׁלַיִם עִיר קָדְשֶׁךָ וְזִכְרוֹן כָּל
עַמְּךָ בֵּית יִשְׂרָאֵל לְפָנֶיךָ, לִפְלֵיטָה לְטוֹבָה לְחֵן וּלְחֶסֶד
וּלְרַחֲמִים לְחַיִּים וּלְשָׁלוֹם בְּיוֹם חַג הַמַּצּוֹת הַזֶּה. זָכְרֵנוּ יְיָ
אֱלֹהֵינוּ בּוֹ לְטוֹבָה, וּפָקְדֵנוּ בוֹ לִבְרָכָה, וְהוֹשִׁיעֵנוּ בוֹ לְחַיִּים
טוֹבִים. וּבִדְבַר יְשׁוּעָה וְרַחֲמִים חוּס וְחָנֵּנוּ וְרַחֵם עָלֵינוּ
וְהוֹשִׁיעֵנוּ כִּי אֵלֶיךָ עֵינֵינוּ כִּי אֵל מֶלֶךְ חַנּוּן וְרַחוּם אָתָּה:
וּבְנֵה יְרוּשָׁלַיִם עִיר הַקֹּדֶשׁ בִּמְהֵרָה בְיָמֵינוּ בָּרוּךְ אַתָּה יְיָ
בּוֹנֵה בְרַחֲמָיו יְרוּשָׁלָיִם. אָמֵן:

And rebuild Yerushalayim
ובנה ירושלים

Last night I prayed by the Holy Wall, and I asked the Almighty all my questions. "If You are the One who loves the world, if You are the One who cares for every little creature, if You are the One that gave us the Holy Land, where were You when six million walked into the gas chambers? Where are You when people break each other's hearts? Where are You when homes are destroyed?" And I looked up to Heaven and I heard the angels singing, and I knew the Almighty is on His way to do great things. Because whatever happens in the world is only a preparation for this one great thing: *u'vneih Yerushalayim*, the rebuilding of Jerusalem.

What do you think about when you eat? Some people forget the whole world when they eat. There are holy, deep people who have different thoughts than ordinary people. After they eat they *bentsch* and say, "Thank you, God, for feeding me, for sustaining me. Thank you for the Holy Land." But then they're left with one big question, because they're the kind of people who, while they ate, remembered all the hungry people. They remem-

Our God and God of our fathers, may the remembrance and consideration of us; the remembrance of our fathers; the remembrance of Mashiach, son of David, Your servant; the remembrance of Yerushalayim, the City of Your Holiness; the remembrance of all Your people, the House of Israel, go up, and come, and reach, and be seen, and be favored, and be heard, and be considered, and be remembered before You, for deliverance, for goodness, for grace, for kindness, for compassion, for life, and for peace, on this day of the Festival of Matzos. Remember us, Hashem our God, on this day for goodness; consider us on it for blessing; and save us on it for life. And with Your word of salvation and mercy, pity us and be gracious and compassionate with us, and save us, for our eyes are turned to You, because You are a gracious and compassionate God and King.

And rebuild Yerushalayim, the holy city, soon in our days. Blessed are You, Hashem, Who rebuilds Yerushalayim (in His mercy). Amen.

---

bered all the people who are heartbroken. So now they ask the Almighty, "If it's true that You're feeding the world, why is the Holy Temple destroyed? Why are so many people hungry? Why are so many people standing on the corners of so many streets? Why are hearts broken, windows broken, doors broken?"

It's only natural to say, "Almighty, I have one request for you. There's only one way to rebuild the whole world: *u'vneih Yerushalayim*, rebuild the Holy City, the capital of the world, the capital of everything that's beautiful

בָּרוּךְ אַתָּה יְיָ אֱלֹהֵינוּ מֶלֶךְ הָעוֹלָם הָאֵל אָבִינוּ מַלְכֵּנוּ
אַדִּירֵנוּ בּוֹרְאֵנוּ גּוֹאֲלֵנוּ יוֹצְרֵנוּ קְדוֹשֵׁנוּ קְדוֹשׁ יַעֲקֹב רוֹעֵנוּ
רוֹעֵה יִשְׂרָאֵל הַמֶּלֶךְ הַטּוֹב וְהַמֵּטִיב לַכֹּל שֶׁבְּכָל יוֹם וָיוֹם
הוּא הֵטִיב הוּא מֵטִיב הוּא יֵיטִיב לָנוּ הוּא גְמָלָנוּ הוּא גוֹמְלֵנוּ
הוּא יִגְמְלֵנוּ לָעַד לְחֵן וּלְחֶסֶד וּלְרַחֲמִים וּלְרֶוַח הַצָּלָה
וְהַצְלָחָה בְּרָכָה וִישׁוּעָה נֶחָמָה פַּרְנָסָה וְכַלְכָּלָה וְרַחֲמִים
וְחַיִּים וְשָׁלוֹם וְכָל טוֹב וּמִכָּל טוּב לְעוֹלָם אַל יְחַסְּרֵנוּ:

and holy in the world. *Bimheirah b'yameinu,* in our days, let us be there."

הוא יגמלנו לעד   He will be bountiful to us forever

The *heilige* Rebbe Moshe Leib of Sassov, who was famous for the great love he had for every Jew, left this world and went up to heaven. When he came before the Heavenly Court, they announced that he could enter Paradise without delay.

But the Rebbe surprised them. He announced, "I'm not going to go there, and I'll tell you why. If it's true that God wants me to live in heavenly bliss, filled with joy and everlasting content, then all of the *Yidden* have to come into Paradise with me. Just think, what kind of pleasure could I take in Paradise as long as one *yiddele* is in pain? How could I live in bliss, knowing that another *Yid* is in hell? So I'm telling you, if you want to give me my heavenly reward there's only one way you can do it. You'll have to take all the *Yidden* out of Hell."

The Heavenly Court thought it over, and this was their decision. If there had ever once been a time that a Jew needed the Sassover Rebbe and the Rebbe hadn't been there to help him, then his merit would not be enough, and the *Yidden* would have to stay in Hell. But if he had never once missed a chance to help, if his whole life long he had never turned down even one person, then his merit was so great that for his sake all the *Yidden* could come out of Hell, just to make him happy. And that is how the Sassover took

Blessed are You, Hashem our God, King of the Universe, God our Father, our King, our Mighty One, our Creator, our Redeemer, our Maker, our Holy One, the Holy One of Jacob; our Shepherd, the Shepherd of Israel, the King Who is good and Who continually does good to all. For day after day He did good, He does good, and He will do good to us. He was bountiful to us, He is bountiful to us, and He will be bountiful to us forever, with grace and with kindness and with mercy, and with relief, rescue and success, blessing and salvation, consolation, sustenance and support, and with mercy and life and peace, and all good; and may He never deprive us of all good things.

everyone with him into God's eternal bliss.

הָרַחֲמָן הוּא יִמְלֹךְ עָלֵינוּ לְעוֹלָם וָעֶד. הָרַחֲמָן הוּא יִתְבָּרַךְ
בַּשָּׁמַיִם וּבָאָרֶץ. הָרַחֲמָן הוּא יִשְׁתַּבַּח לְדוֹר דּוֹרִים וְיִתְפָּאַר
בָּנוּ לָעַד וּלְנֵצַח נְצָחִים וְיִתְהַדַּר בָּנוּ לָעַד וּלְעוֹלְמֵי עוֹלָמִים.
הָרַחֲמָן הוּא יְפַרְנְסֵנוּ בְּכָבוֹד. הָרַחֲמָן הוּא יִשְׁבּוֹר עֻלֵנוּ מֵעַל
צַוָּארֵנוּ וְהוּא יוֹלִיכֵנוּ קוֹמְמִיּוּת לְאַרְצֵנוּ. הָרַחֲמָן הוּא יִשְׁלַח
לָנוּ בְּרָכָה מְרֻבָּה בַּבַּיִת הַזֶּה וְעַל שֻׁלְחָן זֶה שֶׁאָכַלְנוּ עָלָיו.
הָרַחֲמָן הוּא יִשְׁלַח לָנוּ אֶת אֵלִיָּהוּ הַנָּבִיא זָכוּר לַטּוֹב וִיבַשֶּׂר
לָנוּ בְּשׂוֹרוֹת טוֹבוֹת יְשׁוּעוֹת וְנֶחָמוֹת. הָרַחֲמָן הוּא יְבָרֵךְ
אֶת (אָבִי מוֹרִי) בַּעַל הַבַּיִת הַזֶּה וְאֶת (אִמִּי מוֹרָתִי) בַּעֲלַת
הַבַּיִת הַזֶּה. אוֹתָם וְאֶת בֵּיתָם וְאֶת זַרְעָם וְאֶת כָּל אֲשֶׁר
לָהֶם. (אִם הוּא סָמוּךְ עַל שֻׁלְחָן עַצְמוֹ אוֹמֵר: הָרַחֲמָן הוּא
יְבָרֵךְ אוֹתִי (וְאֶת אָבִי מוֹרִי וְאֶת אִמִּי מוֹרָתִי) וְאֶת אִשְׁתִּי
וְאֶת זַרְעִי וְכָל אֲשֶׁר לִי) אוֹתָנוּ וְאֶת כָּל אֲשֶׁר לָנוּ כְּמוֹ
שֶׁנִּתְבָּרְכוּ אֲבוֹתֵינוּ אַבְרָהָם יִצְחָק וְיַעֲקֹב בַּכֹּל מִכֹּל כֹּל,
כֵּן יְבָרֵךְ אוֹתָנוּ כֻּלָּנוּ יַחַד בִּבְרָכָה שְׁלֵמָה וְנֹאמַר אָמֵן:

May He send us Eliyahu   הוא ישלח לנו את אליהו הנביא

There's a piece of Torah that the *heilige* Vizhnitzer Rebbe said: Everybody knows that before the Mashiach can come, first Eliyahu Hanavi has to come, "*viyevaser lanu besoros tovos*, and he'll bring us good tidings, salvation, and consolation." In other words, he'll let us know Mashiach is coming. But if that's so, how do we say "*bimheirah yavo eileinu **im** Mashiach*, may he come to us quickly **with** the Mashiach." We just said that he comes beforehand, not with him!

So the Vizhnitzer Rebbe says like this: the prophet said, "*b'itah achishe-nah*, in its proper time I will hasten the Redemption." If it's *b'itah*, if this is the right time for Mashiach to come, then Eliyahu Hanavi comes first to let us know Mashiach is coming. If it's *achishenah*, if he comes early because

The compassionate One! May He be king over us forever. The compassionate One! May He be blessed in heaven and on earth. The compassionate One! May He be praised throughout all generations; may He be glorified through us forever and for all eternities; and be honored through us forever and for all eternity. The compassionate One! May He sustain us in honor. The compassionate One! May He break the yoke of oppression from our necks and lead us with raised heads to our Land. The compassionate One! May He send abundant blessing to this house and upon this table at which we have eaten. The compassionate One! May He send us Eliyahu, the well-remembered prophet, and let him bring us good tidings, salvations, and consolations.

Guests say the words in the brackets. Children at their parents' table add the words in parentheses:

The compassionate One! May He bless me, my wife [husband], and my children, and all that is mine. [May He bless (my father and teacher) the master of this house, and (my mother and teacher) the lady of this house – them, their house, their family, and all that is theirs.] And may He bless us and all that is ours – just as our forefathers Avraham, Yitzchak and Yaakov were blessed in everything, from everything, and with everything. So may He bless us all together with a perfect blessing, and let us say: Amen!

בַּמָּרוֹם יְלַמְּדוּ (עֲלֵיהֶם וְ)עָלֵינוּ זְכוּת שֶׁתְּהֵא לְמִשְׁמֶרֶת שָׁלוֹם. וְנִשָּׂא בְרָכָה מֵאֵת יְיָ וּצְדָקָה מֵאֱלֹהֵי יִשְׁעֵנוּ וְנִמְצָא חֵן וְשֵׂכֶל טוֹב בְּעֵינֵי אֱלֹהִים וְאָדָם:

On Shabbos add:

הָרַחֲמָן הוּא יַנְחִילֵנוּ יוֹם שֶׁכֻּלּוֹ שַׁבָּת וּמְנוּחָה לְחַיֵּי הָעוֹלָמִים:

הָרַחֲמָן הוּא יַנְחִילֵנוּ יוֹם שֶׁכֻּלּוֹ טוֹב יוֹם שֶׁכֻּלּוֹ אָרוּךְ יוֹם שֶׁצַּדִּיקִים יוֹשְׁבִים וְעַטְרוֹתֵיהֶם בְּרָאשֵׁיהֶם וְנֶהֱנִים מִזִּיו הַשְּׁכִינָה וִיהִי חֶלְקֵנוּ עִמָּהֶם:

הָרַחֲמָן הוּא יְזַכֵּנוּ לִימוֹת הַמָּשִׁיחַ וּלְחַיֵּי הָעוֹלָם הַבָּא. מַגְדִּל יְשׁוּעוֹת מַלְכּוֹ וְעֹשֶׂה חֶסֶד לִמְשִׁיחוֹ לְדָוִד וּלְזַרְעוֹ עַד עוֹלָם: עֹשֶׂה שָׁלוֹם בִּמְרוֹמָיו הוּא יַעֲשֶׂה שָׁלוֹם עָלֵינוּ וְעַל כָּל יִשְׂרָאֵל וְאִמְרוּ אָמֵן:

Yidden do teshuvah and we have the privilege — may we all have it! — to bring Mashiach one step closer to the world, then the *Ribbono shel Olam* brings him suddenly, because if we do teshuvah there's no time for Eliyahu Hanavi to come first. So we say *bimheirah yavo eileinu,* let him come quickly. Master of the world, have mercy! Let it be tonight that he comes with the Mashiach ben David.

On high, may merit be invoked upon them and upon us, for an enduring peace. May we carry with us a blessing from Hashem and righteousness from the God of our salvation, and find favor and good understanding in the eyes of God and man.

On Shabbos add:

The compassionate One! May He cause us to inherit the day which will be completely Shabbos and rest for eternal life.

The compassionate One! May He cause us to inherit the day which is completely good: the everlasting day, the day when the just will sit with crowns on their heads, enjoying the glow of the Divine Presence – and may our portion be with them!

The compassionate One! May He make us worthy of the days of Mashiach and the life of the World to Come. He is a tower of salvation for His king and does kindness to His anointed, to David and to his descendants forever. He Who makes peace in His heights will make peace upon us and upon all Israel. And say Amen!

יְראוּ אֶת יְיָ קְדֹשָׁיו כִּי אֵין מַחְסוֹר לִירֵאָיו: כְּפִירִים רָשׁוּ וְרָעֵבוּ
וְדֹרְשֵׁי יְיָ לֹא יַחְסְרוּ כָל טוֹב: הוֹדוּ לַיְיָ כִּי טוֹב כִּי לְעוֹלָם
חַסְדּוֹ: פּוֹתֵחַ אֶת יָדֶךָ וּמַשְׂבִּיעַ לְכָל חַי רָצוֹן: בָּרוּךְ הַגֶּבֶר
אֲשֶׁר יִבְטַח בַּיְיָ וְהָיָה יְיָ מִבְטַחוֹ: נַעַר הָיִיתִי גַּם זָקַנְתִּי וְלֹא
רָאִיתִי צַדִּיק נֶעֱזָב וְזַרְעוֹ מְבַקֶּשׁ לָחֶם יְיָ עֹז לְעַמּוֹ יִתֵּן יְיָ
יְבָרֵךְ אֶת עַמּוֹ בַשָּׁלוֹם:

ה' עוז לעמו יתן   **Hashem will give strength to His people**

God, please give strength to your people. You know, friends, sometimes
we don't know where our strength will come from any more. Let me tell you
about a *Yid* who came to the Holy Land. He fought in 1948, and again in
1956. He had two sons, two holy sons. In the war of 1967 one son left this
world. He sanctified God's name, he gave his life for the Holy Land. On Yom
Kippur 1973 the second son joined his father Abraham in Heaven.

I heard this story from the person who has the job of telling parents if,
God forbid, their children die. He told me he just didn't have the strength
any more. He drove around the block five times. How can you tell parents
such a thing? But regardless, finally he made himself strong. He walked up
to this *Chassidishe Yid* and said to him, "I'm so sorry to tell you, the son you
had left is also gone." You know what this *Yiddele* did? God gave him so
much strength from Heaven; he took a little wine and said, "*L'chaim*, my
holy son. I envy you that you gave your life for the Holy Land." He said
L'chaim to his wife too: "You were privileged to have two holy sons who gave
their lives for the Holy Land." May Hashem give strength to His people; may
Hashem bless His people with peace.

Revere Hashem, you His holy ones, for those who revere Him lack nothing. Young lions are poor and hunger, but those who seek Hashem will not lack any good. Give thanks to Hashem, for He is good, for His kindness endures forever. You open Your hand and satisfy the desire of every living thing. Blessed is the man who trusts in Hashem – then Hashem will be his security. I was a youth and also have aged, and I have not seen a righteous man forsaken and his children begging for bread. Hashem will give [inner] strength to His people; Hashem will bless His people with peace.

The blessing over wine is recited and the third cup is drunk while reclining on the left side.

בָּרוּךְ אַתָּה יְיָ אֱלֹהֵינוּ מֶלֶךְ הָעוֹלָם בּוֹרֵא פְּרִי הַגָּפֶן:

We pour a cup in honor of Eliyahu Hanavi. It is usually poured by the leader of the Seder. While the Cup of Eliyahu is on the table, the door is opened for the prophet Eliyahu. Everyone rises and says the following paragraph:

שְׁפֹךְ חֲמָתְךָ אֶל הַגּוֹיִם אֲשֶׁר לֹא יְדָעוּךָ וְעַל מַמְלָכוֹת אֲשֶׁר בְּשִׁמְךָ לֹא קָרָאוּ. כִּי אָכַל אֶת יַעֲקֹב וְאֶת נָוֵהוּ הֵשַׁמּוּ. שְׁפָךְ עֲלֵיהֶם זַעְמֶךָ וַחֲרוֹן אַפְּךָ יַשִּׂיגֵם. תִּרְדֹּף בְּאַף וְתַשְׁמִידֵם מִתַּחַת שְׁמֵי יְיָ:

The Cup of Eliyahu   כוסו של אליהו

Our spirits are so high. At the end of the Seder it's clear to us that Eliyahu Hanavi has to come in. A lot of people today think that maybe we need a different Haggadah. Sadly enough, most of these people don't even speak Hebrew. They have no idea what the Haggadah is really about. Let me just share with you what the *heilige* Radziminer Rebbe said he heard in Pshischa. They said there that the Haggadah was composed by Eliyahu Hanavi, the one who lives forever.

On Seder night, death and everything that's unholy is wiped out from the world. The Tree of Knowledge brought death to the world, and it made everyone either good or bad. The Tree of Knowledge is all head, but the Tree of Life is heart. A pure heart is a vessel for the utmost joy — *ul'yishrei leiv simchah*. If I'm completely alive, I can love everything.

If you love someone with your heart — I don't mean emotionally, but deep inside — nothing can change it. When God in His great mercy revives the dead, all the people we loved before, we'll still love them, even though thousands of years have gone by. Imagine if you're very tired, you're about to go to sleep, and then the person you really love comes in to visit. At that moment you get a new infusion of life. Even greater: imagine a person's on his deathbed; he's about to die, and the person he loves comes in. He can't die then, he's so connected to the Tree of Life.

We have to teach our children first of all to love the world; we have to show them the beauty of it. If we teach them from the Tree of Knowledge

The Third Cup

The blessing over wine is recited and the third cup is drunk while reclining on the left side.

Blessed are You, Hashem, our God, King of the universe, Creator of the fruit of the vine.

We pour a cup in honor of Eliyahu Hanavi. It is usually poured by the leader of the Seder. While the Cup of Eliyahu is on the table, the door is opened for the prophet Eliyahu. Everyone rises and says the following paragraph:

Pour Your wrath upon the nations that do not know You and upon the kingdoms that do not cry out in Your Name. For they have devoured Yaakov and destroyed his habitation. Pour Your anger upon them and let Your wrath overtake them. Pursue them with wrath and annihilate them from beneath the heavens of Hashem.

first, we're bringing death to the world. If I tell them, "There are so many criminals in the world, every third person you meet is a criminal," then what will happen when they're sitting in class? They'll look at their classmates and think, "This one is bright, this one is stupid; he's ugly, he's terrible." First you have to connect them to the Tree of Life.

People, nations, don't all think the same way. They're all so different. They can only make peace by holding on to the Tree of Life and saying, "We don't mind how you think, what your beliefs are. We love you."

The Spoler Zaide was called "Zaide" because he loved everyone like a grandfather. They say the Baal Shem Tov put his hand on the Spoler Zaide's heart when he was still a young boy and blessed him to have a real Jewish heart.

Pesach comes after Purim. On Purim we erase Haman's name: we wipe out evil. There's no Tree of Knowledge any more. I'm so drunk, I'm only aware of things that are real. I don't give a darn about theories — I know that an apple is an apple, a banana is a banana, and wine is wine.

Only on Purim you can send *shallach manos*. During the year, if I bring you a gift of a banana and an apple, you'd say, "A banana costs 15 cents and an apple 12 cents. What kind of chutzpah to give me these things!" This is what happens when you eat from the Tree of Knowledge: you measure, this is good, this is bad. You buy me a house in Monaco, or you donate two million dollars to my yeshivah — then you're okay. But on Purim it's the Tree of Life. I don't measure, because my head isn't running the show any more. I love with my heart. So whatever you give me, thank you.

After Purim can come the Seder night. We know how to use our heads, but now we're above the head. We're heavenly; our hearts are open. I look at every human being, every Jew, and see God's image — it's so much deeper than a question of good or bad. I look at my children, and I see God's face; I'm back in paradise.

Eliyahu Hanavi comes at the end of the Seder. Every adult and every child goes out to greet Elijah the Prophet, and sometimes we stand there for infinite time. At this moment all the gates of Heaven are open; you can ask Him for everything. The most important thing, and my blessing to you is that you'll do it: to hold your children's hands while you wait for Eliyahu Hanavi.

Sometimes you want to send a message to someone you love, but you don't know where they are. But then there are always two who know where every *Yid* is: *HaKadosh baruch Hu,* and our friend Eliyahu Hanavi. You and I know that Eliyahu lives forever — of course we know it, because he's every Jew's best friend. Through him we're sending messages to all of Israel who still haven't come to the Holy Land. Some of the *Yidden* are so far away, physically, mentally, spiritually. Eliyahu, please bring them back.

I want to share with you two Eliyahu Hanavi stories, one from a long time ago, and one from today.

The *heilige* Rebbe Nachum Tchernobiler all his life collected money for poor brides. The holy Baal Shem Tov one time told him, "In a village in Russia there are ten brides, and I need ten thousand rubles to marry them off." Rebbe Nachum decided to go to Brod, Poland, a big city with a lot of rich Jews. Hopefully, with God's help he'd collect the ten thousand rubles.

The story turns a bit sad now. Rebbe Nachum was in Brod for two weeks and he didn't collect even one penny. In the end he walked right out of the city, fuming with anger — he was angry at God. He walked along the road, then he stopped under a tree and started to talk to God about his anger: "*Ribbono shel Olam*, Master of the world, if I came to collect money for myself, You have the right to help me or not help me. But it's not for me; I'll never see those ten brides, I don't even know who they are. I did it for You, *Ribbono shel Olam*. Why don't You help me? I'm so angry! I'm going home to take care of my own children; I'm not collecting any more to help poor brides." He was angry at God, but at the same time he was broken inside, because he didn't want to be angry. He was torn apart.

Suddenly he saw the police coming. They were holding a little Jew between them, and the *Yiddele* was dancing while they held him. He was singing, glowing with joy. Here Rebbe Nachum was free, and he was sitting and crying; and this *Yiddele*, who was obviously a thief who'd been caught, was glowing with joy. Rebbe Nachum said to him, "My dear Jew, who are you?" He opened his eyes very wide and said, "What? You don't know me? I'm Moishele the *ganav*, the most famous thief in Brod."

Rebbe Nachum said, "I'll tell you the truth, I was in Brod for just a few days, so I didn't have the great pleasure of meeting you yet. But I'm so glad to meet you now." Then he said to him, "Moishele, if you're such a polished thief, how come the police caught you?" He said, "Even the most polished thief gets caught sometimes." The Rebbe said, "Moishele, now you're arrested and you'll be in prison. I hope when you get out you'll stop being a thief." Moishele the *ganav* started laughing, and said, "Do you know what a Jew is all about? A Jew never stops doing what he began to do."

Rebbe Nachum got the message. He went back to the city with great *simchah,* and within a few days he collected the ten thousand rubles. Then he went back to the holy Baal Shem Tov, who looked at him and said, "Nachum, how does Eliyahu Hanavi look when he walks as a thief between policemen?"

You understand, my dear friends: according to our holy tradition, whenever you are about to give up Eliyahu Hanavi comes to give you strength. My blessing for you, brothers and sisters all over the world, is that you let Elijah the prophet come to you. Maybe as a thief, maybe as a policeman, maybe as a Rebbe, but let God send someone to you with a message, to tell you, "Don't give up!"

I had the privilege several years ago to marry a couple — sweet as sugar, holy like the angels in heaven, but very poor. The wedding took place in a loft somewhere in Greenwich Village in New York. They had a jar of herring and a box of matzah; that was it. But *gevalt*, was there joy! Behind me stood a very wealthy woman; her father had millions. She was married for four weeks and then got divorced. It was just two weeks since the divorce, and she was standing behind me watching the *chuppah*. She said to me, "My father spent thirty-five thousand dollars just on the flowers, but there was no joy at the wedding. This couple have just a little bit of herring and matzah, and look at the *simchah*."

By now, thank God, this couple have two children. I met them a few months later, and the wife told me this story. She said, "The last night of *sheva berachos* was held in the Bronx. We were on our way back to Brooklyn, on the subway in New York. Now, you know, the first stop is at 72nd Street and the next express stop is 42nd Street. The whole time my husband was telling me, 'I love you so much, and it really doesn't matter if we're rich or not; but you know something? Tonight I wish I was rich, because the *sheva berachos* are over, and now it's just you and I. So I wish we had enough money to go to a hotel for a few days together.'

"I had a tear in my eye, and I said to my husband, 'I wish so too.' At 72nd Street the door opened and a black man walked in; a good man, but a little drunk. He sat down next to us and said, 'Hey, what's going on here? Are you married, or just fooling around?' We said, 'No, we just got married.' 'Oh, that makes me kind of feel good. I wish I'd been at the wedding.' He talked to us for a while, and before we'd even noticed it the train was at 42nd Street. The man suddenly said 'I'm leaving,' and walked out the door. Then, a split second before the door closed, he threw an envelope into my hand. The door closed, and he was gone. I opened the envelope — a thousand dollars in cash.

הלל

Reciting

the

Hallel

הלל

The fourth cup is poured and we sit down and continue reciting Hallel. Some raise the cup during the recitation of the Hallel.

לֹא לָנוּ יְיָ לֹא לָנוּ כִּי לְשִׁמְךָ תֵּן כָּבוֹד עַל חַסְדְּךָ עַל אֲמִתֶּךָ. לָמָּה יֹאמְרוּ הַגּוֹיִם אַיֵּה נָא אֱלֹהֵיהֶם. וֵאלֹהֵינוּ בַשָּׁמָיִם כֹּל אֲשֶׁר חָפֵץ עָשָׂה. עֲצַבֵּיהֶם כֶּסֶף וְזָהָב מַעֲשֵׂה יְדֵי אָדָם. פֶּה לָהֶם וְלֹא יְדַבֵּרוּ עֵינַיִם לָהֶם וְלֹא יִרְאוּ. אָזְנַיִם לָהֶם וְלֹא יִשְׁמָעוּ אַף לָהֶם וְלֹא יְרִיחוּן. יְדֵיהֶם וְלֹא יְמִישׁוּן רַגְלֵיהֶם וְלֹא יְהַלֵּכוּ לֹא יֶהְגּוּ בִּגְרוֹנָם. כְּמוֹהֶם יִהְיוּ עֹשֵׂיהֶם כֹּל אֲשֶׁר בֹּטֵחַ בָּהֶם. יִשְׂרָאֵל בְּטַח בַּיְיָ עֶזְרָם וּמָגִנָּם הוּא. בֵּית אַהֲרֹן בִּטְחוּ בַיְיָ עֶזְרָם וּמָגִנָּם הוּא. יִרְאֵי יְיָ בִּטְחוּ בַיְיָ עֶזְרָם וּמָגִנָּם הוּא:

הלל

Hallel

I had the privilege to say Hallel on Rosh Chodesh in a prison. *Nebach,* there were young Jewish people, young *chevrah,* twenty or twenty-two years of age. How could I tell them about Hallel? I look at their faces — *nebach,* how can I ask them to say Hallel?

I heard a story from the *heilige* Bobover Rebbe about why R. Mendel Riminover was worthy to study and become a top student of Rebbe Elimelech. There are many versions of this story, and here is one of them:

The Chassidim of Rebbe Elimelech, on the way to Lizhensk, passed by a village. On the balcony of a broken-down house, a little boy was standing and *mamash* dancing like crazy. So they asked him, "Why are you dancing?" He answered, "I'm dancing because I haven't eaten in three days."

They looked at him. He said, "I'll tell you the truth: I'm all of nine years old, and I was so angry at God — *gevalt* was I angry! I said, 'Master of the world, I'm only nine years old; how many *aveiros,* how many mistakes have I made in my life, that I deserve not to eat for three days?' Suddenly I realized: it's true God hasn't fed me for three days, but I have a mother, a father, a brother, and a sister. Our house is not so big, but still, it's a house. I realized I've never thanked God for what I have, so I'm dancing."

The Chassidim walked into the house and said to the parents, "Do you

Hallel

The fourth cup is poured and we sit down and continue reciting Hallel. Some raise the cup during the recitation of the Hallel.

Not for us, Hashem, not for us, but for Your Name's sake give honor, for Your kindness and for Your truth! Why should the nations say, "Where is their God?" Our God is in the heavens; whatever He wills He does. Their idols are silver and gold, the work of human hands. They have a mouth, but cannot speak; they have eyes, but cannot see. They have ears, but cannot hear; they have a nose, but cannot smell. [They have] their hands but cannot feel; [They have] their feet but cannot walk; they cannot utter a sound from their throat. Let those who make them become like them, whoever trusts in them! Israel, trust in Hashem – He is their help and their shield. House of Aaron, trust in Hashem – He is their help and their shield. You who fear Hashem, trust in Hashem – He is their help and their shield.

---

know what kind of son you have? What a *neshamah!* Are you sending him to *cheider* to learn Torah?" They said, "We're too poor to send him to *cheider.*" "Such a *heilige neshamah,*" said the Chassidim, "such a great soul! Please let us take him to Rebbe Elimelech." This boy eventually became R. Mendel Riminover.

So I told this to the people, the *chevrah,* our brothers in prison. I said, "I'm sure you have lots of reasons to be angry at God, and I'm not here to offer excuses for Him. And I wish and bless you to come out of here fast. But maybe, in the meantime, let's dance and thank Him for what we do have."

יְיָ זְכָרָנוּ יְבָרֵךְ יְבָרֵךְ אֶת בֵּית יִשְׂרָאֵל יְבָרֵךְ אֶת בֵּית אַהֲרֹן. יְבָרֵךְ יִרְאֵי יְיָ הַקְּטַנִּים עִם הַגְּדֹלִים. יֹסֵף יְיָ עֲלֵיכֶם עֲלֵיכֶם וְעַל בְּנֵיכֶם. בְּרוּכִים אַתֶּם לַיְיָ עֹשֵׂה שָׁמַיִם וָאָרֶץ. הַשָּׁמַיִם שָׁמַיִם לַיְיָ וְהָאָרֶץ נָתַן לִבְנֵי אָדָם. לֹא הַמֵּתִים יְהַלְלוּ יָהּ וְלֹא כָּל יֹרְדֵי דוּמָה. וַאֲנַחְנוּ נְבָרֵךְ יָהּ מֵעַתָּה וְעַד עוֹלָם הַלְלוּיָהּ:

אָהַבְתִּי כִּי יִשְׁמַע יְיָ אֶת קוֹלִי תַּחֲנוּנָי. כִּי הִטָּה אָזְנוֹ לִי וּבְיָמַי אֶקְרָא. אֲפָפוּנִי חֶבְלֵי מָוֶת וּמְצָרֵי שְׁאוֹל מְצָאוּנִי צָרָה וְיָגוֹן אֶמְצָא. וּבְשֵׁם יְיָ אֶקְרָא אָנָּה יְיָ מַלְּטָה נַפְשִׁי. חַנּוּן יְיָ וְצַדִּיק וֵאלֹהֵינוּ מְרַחֵם. שֹׁמֵר פְּתָאִים יְיָ דַּלּוֹתִי וְלִי יְהוֹשִׁיעַ. שׁוּבִי נַפְשִׁי לִמְנוּחָיְכִי כִּי יְיָ גָּמַל עָלָיְכִי. כִּי חִלַּצְתָּ נַפְשִׁי מִמָּוֶת אֶת עֵינִי מִן דִּמְעָה אֶת רַגְלִי מִדֶּחִי. אֶתְהַלֵּךְ לִפְנֵי יְיָ בְּאַרְצוֹת הַחַיִּים. הֶאֱמַנְתִּי כִּי אֲדַבֵּר אֲנִי עָנִיתִי מְאֹד. אֲנִי אָמַרְתִּי בְחָפְזִי כָּל הָאָדָם כֹּזֵב:

Israel, trust in Hashem
ישראל בטח בה'

You know, friends, sometimes it makes me sad, and yet sometimes it makes me happy: Israel has no friends in the world. The Holy Land, the holy people of Israel, are all alone. *Am l'vadad yishkon*, we are truly a people that dwells alone. But you know what we have? *Yisrael b'tach baShem*, we have One friend in heaven, and we can trust in Him.

The pains of death surrounded me
אפפוני חבלי מות

About a hundred and twenty years ago there lived a rich Jew in Odessa who was a banker. At least, he thought he was rich. One day he told his accountant, "Let me look at the books." When he did, he realized that unless

Hashem, Who has remembered us, will bless – He will bless the House of Israel; He will bless the House of Aharon; He will bless those who revere Hashem, the small as well as the great. Hashem will increase you, you and your children. Blessed are you to Hashem, maker of heaven and earth. The heavens are Hashem's heavens, but the earth He has given to mankind. The dead cannot praise God, nor any who go down into silence; but we will bless God from this time forth and forever: Halleluyah!

I love it when Hashem hears my voice, my supplications. For He has inclined His ear to me, and in my own days I will call Him. The pains of death surrounded me, and the confines of the grave have found me; trouble and sorrow I found. Then I would call the Name of Hashem: "Please Hashem, deliver my soul." Gracious is Hashem and righteous; our God is merciful. Hashem watches over the foolish; I was brought low, but He saved me. Return, my soul, to your resting place, for Hashem has been kind to you. For You have rescued my soul from death, my eyes from tears, my feet from stumbling. I shall walk before Hashem in the lands of the living. I had faith even while speaking of how I suffer so much, [even though] I said in haste, "All mankind is deceitful."

he put two million rubles into his bank he would go bankrupt in four days.

Today if someone is bankrupt, he declares bankruptcy and that's all he does. Then he goes on vacation to Switzerland, and sends letters to all the people he owes money to: "I wish you were here, I'm having a great time." In those days, if you declared bankruptcy you were on the next train to Siberia. But, he thought, he needn't be so desperate. "I have enough credit, I'll just borrow from another bank."

To make it short, he found he couldn't get credit. By the second day he decided he had to commit suicide in order not to go to Siberia and put his family to shame. But he thought, "I can't commit suicide near my wife and children, I'll do it in the synagogue." He went to the synagogue and put the poison on a top shelf under one of the books; but then he went home: he decided he'd leave himself two more days. He tried and tried to get the two million rubles. He couldn't get it.

On the fourth night he thought, "It's heartbreaking, but what can you do?" He told his wife after dinner, "I have to do some errands," and he went to the synagogue. There was no electric light then, just candles, so he put the candle on the table and reached up with his hand to take the poison out from under the book. He was, *nebach*, trembling so much that the book that was on top of the poison fell down.

And what book was it? The teachings of Rebbe Nachman, the holy master from Breslav. Now, usually on the first page of a book it says the name of the book and the name of the author. But those who printed Rebbe Nachman's Torah decided to write on the first page: *Rebbe Nachman, our holy master, says, "Don't ever give up!"* And only on the second page it says, "These are teachings of our holy master Rebbe Nachman."

This book fell down and automatically the banker bent down to pick it up. The book had opened, and he looked and it said: *Rebbe Nachman says, "Don't ever give up!"*

He sat down at the table with the book and said slowly, "Master of the world, is this a message from you? I won't commit suicide tonight. I'll wait another day. But please don't disappoint me." So he sat there, and just looked at the words, "Don't give up!" all night long.

On the fifth day, each time there was a knock on the door he was sure it was the police. It wasn't. For three more nights he went to the synagogue and just stared at those words all night.

On the seventh day he got a letter from a bank in Holland. It said, "A thousand pardons, sir! Seven years ago we took a loan from you and we completely forgot to pay it back. Now we are paying back with interest." It came to over two million rubles. That night he went to the synagogue again, his heart full of joy. This was the first time he turned to the second page of the holy book. There it said, "These are the teachings of the master Rebbe

Nachman, the great-grandson of the holy Baal Shem Tov." He turned another page, and he found the teaching of "Happy are those that walk in the way of God."

He was so tired from the previous nights that soon he fell asleep on the book. In his dream he saw a youngish man, maybe thirty-eight, with ear locks and a small beard. He asked, "Who are you?" The man said, "My name is Nachman, and you're learning my book. A hundred years ago, when I was shouting never to give up, I was praying for you." The man asked, "Holy master, what should I do now?" Rebbe Nachman answered, "I'll tell you. Sell your bank and go to the Holy Land. Please print my book in the Holy Land."

I want you to know, I met an old Breslaver Chassid, ninety years old. He is a student of that banker from Odessa, who turned him on to Rebbe Nachman. From him I heard this story. That means, I heard the story from someone who knew the banker. I bless you, friends, don't ever give up. Don't ever be sad. If you see someone sad and desperate, give him strength.

שובי נפשי   Return, my soul

Master of the world, let my soul be at peace again. Let me be filled with joy again. *Ki Hashem gamal alaykhi*, Hashem has given me such a gift. Thank You for the gift you gave me; I know I don't deserve it. Thank You for the heavenly soul in me. *Ki chilatzta nafshi mimaves*, You saved me from death. *Gevalt*, all of us, we look back at what happened to us just over the last year, and — Master of the world, You redeemed us and our children from death a thousand times. *Es eini min dim'ah*, You spared my eyes from tears. So much pain You could have given me, but You took it away so my eyes wouldn't weep. *Es ragli midechi*, You spared my feet from slipping. So many stones You cleared away for me so I wouldn't stumble.

את עיני מן דמעה   My eyes from tears

For the Rebbes — our Masters, our giants — from this world to the other world was a very short distance. After R. Yitzchak Vorker died, his son, R. Mendele, was very worried. He'd been sure that his father would come and talk to him in a dream, and as yet he hadn't heard from him. So he went to his father's best friend, the Kotzker Rebbe.

מָה אָשִׁיב לַייָ כָּל תַּגְמוּלוֹהִי עָלָי. כּוֹס יְשׁוּעוֹת אֶשָּׂא וּבְשֵׁם יְיָ אֶקְרָא. נְדָרַי לַייָ אֲשַׁלֵּם נֶגְדָה נָּא לְכָל עַמּוֹ. יָקָר בְּעֵינֵי יְיָ הַמָּוְתָה לַחֲסִידָיו. אָנָּה יְיָ כִּי אֲנִי עַבְדֶּךָ אֲנִי עַבְדְּךָ בֶּן אֲמָתֶךָ פִּתַּחְתָּ לְמוֹסֵרָי. לְךָ אֶזְבַּח זֶבַח תּוֹדָה וּבְשֵׁם יְיָ אֶקְרָא. נְדָרַי לַייָ אֲשַׁלֵּם נֶגְדָה נָּא לְכָל עַמּוֹ. בְּחַצְרוֹת בֵּית יְיָ בְּתוֹכֵכִי יְרוּשָׁלַיִם הַלְלוּיָהּ:

הַלְלוּ אֶת יְיָ כָּל גּוֹיִם שַׁבְּחוּהוּ כָּל הָאֻמִּים. כִּי גָבַר עָלֵינוּ חַסְדּוֹ וֶאֱמֶת יְיָ לְעוֹלָם הַלְלוּיָהּ:

If three people are present, the leader recites each verse and the others repeat after him.

הוֹדוּ לַייָ כִּי טוֹב   כִּי לְעוֹלָם חַסְדּוֹ.

יֹאמַר נָא יִשְׂרָאֵל   כִּי לְעוֹלָם חַסְדּוֹ.

יֹאמְרוּ נָא בֵית אַהֲרֹן   כִּי לְעוֹלָם חַסְדּוֹ.

יֹאמְרוּ נָא יִרְאֵי יְיָ   כִּי לְעוֹלָם חַסְדּוֹ

The Rebbe said to him, "To tell you the truth, I was also very worried that he didn't come to me and tell me what is happening to him in the other world. So I went to him. I went to all the palaces: the palace of Rashi, the Rambam, Rebbe Akiva. They told me he'd been there, but he'd left. I asked the angels, 'Do you know where my best friend, the holy R. Yitzchak Vorker, is?' They said, 'You have to go through a very dark forest, and at the end of the forest you'll find him.' I summoned up all my energy, I walked through the forest, and at the end was a great ocean. I never before heard waves crying in such a way. And there was my friend Yitzchak, leaning on a stick, not taking his eyes off the ocean. I said, 'Yitzchak, my best friend, what are you doing here?' He said to me, 'Mendel, do you recognize this ocean?' I said, 'No, what is it?' He said, 'Mendele, this is the ocean of tears of God's holy people, of all of Israel. I have sworn I will not leave the shore of this ocean until God has dried all the tears.'"

My friends, many times we come to houses where children are crying. Their parents tell them to act grown up and to stop crying, or perhaps they

What can I return to Hashem for all His kindnesses to me? I will raise the cup of salvation and call the Name of Hashem. My vows to Hashem I will pay, in the presence of all His people. Harsh in Hashem's eyes is the death of His devout ones. Please, Hashem, for I am Your servant, I am Your servant the son of Your handmaid: You have released my bonds. To You I will offer thanksgiving offerings, and I will call the name of Hashem. My vows to Hashem I will pay, in the presence of all His people, in the courtyards of the House of Hashem, in your midst, Yerushalayim: Halleluyah!

Praise Hashem, all nations, praise Him, all peoples! For His kindness has overwhelmed us, and the truth of Hashem is forever: Halleluyah!

If three people are present, the leader recites each one of the following verses and the others respond by repeating the first verse and the verse that was just said by the leader.

Give thanks to Hashem for He is good: His kindness endures forever!

Let Israel say: His kindness endures forever!

Let the House of Aharon say: His kindness endures forever!

Let those who revere Hashem say: His kindness endures forever!

are not even paying attention to the children's tears. I bless you to stay there and not leave until the One, the Only One, dries their tears. When children are crying, their tears reach Heaven. Don't ever walk away.

מִן הַמֵּצַר קָרָאתִי יָּהּ עָנָנִי בַמֶּרְחָב יָהּ. יְיָ לִי לֹא אִירָא מַה יַּעֲשֶׂה לִי אָדָם. יְיָ לִי בְּעֹזְרָי וַאֲנִי אֶרְאֶה בְשֹׂנְאָי. טוֹב לַחֲסוֹת בַּיְיָ מִבְּטֹחַ בָּאָדָם. טוֹב לַחֲסוֹת בַּיְיָ מִבְּטֹחַ בִּנְדִיבִים. כָּל גּוֹיִם סְבָבוּנִי בְּשֵׁם יְיָ כִּי אֲמִילַם. סַבּוּנִי גַם סְבָבוּנִי בְּשֵׁם יְיָ כִּי אֲמִילַם. סַבּוּנִי כִדְבֹרִים דֹּעֲכוּ כְּאֵשׁ קוֹצִים בְּשֵׁם יְיָ כִּי אֲמִילַם. דָּחֹה דְחִיתַנִי לִנְפֹּל וַיְיָ עֲזָרָנִי. עָזִּי וְזִמְרָת יָהּ וַיְהִי לִי לִישׁוּעָה. קוֹל רִנָּה וִישׁוּעָה בְּאָהֳלֵי צַדִּיקִים יְמִין יְיָ עֹשָׂה חָיִל. יְמִין יְיָ רוֹמֵמָה יְמִין יְיָ עֹשָׂה חָיִל. לֹא אָמוּת כִּי אֶחְיֶה וַאֲסַפֵּר מַעֲשֵׂי יָהּ. יַסֹּר יִסְּרַנִּי יָּהּ וְלַמָּוֶת לֹא נְתָנָנִי. פִּתְחוּ לִי שַׁעֲרֵי צֶדֶק אָבֹא בָם אוֹדֶה יָהּ. זֶה הַשַּׁעַר לַיְיָ צַדִּיקִים יָבֹאוּ בוֹ. אוֹדְךָ כִּי עֲנִיתָנִי וַתְּהִי לִי לִישׁוּעָה. אוֹדְךָ: אֶבֶן מָאֲסוּ הַבּוֹנִים הָיְתָה לְרֹאשׁ פִּנָּה. אֶבֶן: מֵאֵת יְיָ הָיְתָה זֹּאת הִיא נִפְלָאת בְּעֵינֵינוּ. מֵאֵת: זֶה הַיּוֹם עָשָׂה יְיָ נָגִילָה וְנִשְׂמְחָה בוֹ. זֶה:

אבן מאסו הבונים   The stone despised by the builders

In the *Beis Hamikdash*, the Holy Temple, one stone was big, one stone was small, one was round and one was square, but miraculously all the stones fit together. There was one stone, though, *even ma'asu habonim*, that the builders rejected. This stone was the greatest misfit in the world; it didn't fit anywhere, so it was despised by the holy builders. But when the *Beis Hamikdash* was just about finished, the *Kodesh Kodashim*, the Holy of Holies, needed one stone to complete the building, and none of the stones available fit.

Finally somebody remembered that castaway stone. All of a sudden, *haysah l'rosh pinah*, it became the cornerstone; because the castaway stone was the only stone that fit. It was now the crown of the building. The Midrash says, "*Amar David Hamelech*, King David said before God, 'We

From the straits did I call upon God; God answered me with abundance. Hashem is with me, I am not afraid; what can man do to me? Hashem is with me through my helpers, and I can face my enemy. It is better to hope in Hashem than to trust in man. It is better to hope in Hashem than to trust in nobles. All the nations surround me; in the Name of Hashem I cut them down! They encircle me, they surround me; in the Name of Hashem I cut them down! They encircle me like bees, but they are quenched like a fire of thorns; in the Name of Hashem I cut them down! You pushed me again and again that I might fall, but Hashem helped me. God is my strength and my song, and He was for me, my salvation. The sound of rejoicing and salvation is in the tents of the righteous: "Hashem's right hand does valiantly!" Hashem's right hand is exalted; Hashem's right hand does valiantly. I shall not die; I shall live and tell about the deeds of God. God has reprimanded me, but He did not let me die. Open for me the gates of righteousness – I will enter them and thank God. This is the gate of Hashem; the righteous will enter through it.

From here on each verse is said twice:

I thank You, for You have answered me and become my salvation. I thank You, for You have answered me and become my salvation. The stone despised by the builders has become the cornerstone. The stone despised by the builders has become the cornerstone. This thing is from Hashem; it is wondrous in our eyes. This thing is from Hashem; it is wondrous in our eyes. This is the day Hashem has made; let us rejoice and be glad on it. This is the day Hashem has made; let us rejoice and be glad on it.

If three people are present, the leader recites each verse and the others repeat after him.

אָנָּא יְיָ הוֹשִׁיעָה נָּא   אָנָּא יְיָ הַצְלִיחָה נָא.

אָנָּא יְיָ הוֹשִׁיעָה נָּא   אָנָּא יְיָ הַצְלִיחָה נָא.

בָּרוּךְ הַבָּא בְּשֵׁם יְיָ בֵּרַכְנוּכֶם מִבֵּית יְיָ. בָּרוּךְ: אֵל יְיָ וַיָּאֶר לָנוּ
אִסְרוּ חַג בַּעֲבֹתִים עַד קַרְנוֹת הַמִּזְבֵּחַ. אֵל: אֵלִי אַתָּה
וְאוֹדֶךָּ אֱלֹהַי אֲרוֹמְמֶךָּ. אֵלִי: הוֹדוּ לַיְיָ כִּי טוֹב כִּי לְעוֹלָם
חַסְדּוֹ. הוֹדוּ:

יְהַלְלוּךָ יְיָ אֱלֹהֵינוּ כָּל מַעֲשֶׂיךָ וַחֲסִידֶיךָ צַדִּיקִים עֹשֵׂי רְצוֹנֶךָ
וְכָל עַמְּךָ בֵּית יִשְׂרָאֵל בְּרִנָּה יוֹדוּ וִיבָרְכוּ וִישַׁבְּחוּ וִיפָאֲרוּ
וִירוֹמְמוּ וְיַעֲרִיצוּ וְיַקְדִּישׁוּ וְיַמְלִיכוּ אֶת שִׁמְךָ מַלְכֵּנוּ תָּמִיד. כִּי
לְךָ טוֹב לְהוֹדוֹת וּלְשִׁמְךָ נָאֶה לְזַמֵּר כִּי מֵעוֹלָם וְעַד עוֹלָם
אַתָּה אֵל:

Yidden are the most despised people of all, *even ma'asu habonim.* We are despised by the whole world. But one day *haysah l'rosh pinah,* we will be the crown of the world."

If three people are present, the leader recites each verse and the others repeat after him.

Please, Hashem, save us, please!

Please, Hashem, save us, please!

Please, Hashem, make us successful, please!

Please, Hashem, make us successful, please!

Blessed is he who comes in the Name of Hashem; we bless you from the House of Hashem. Blessed is he who comes in the Name of Hashem; we bless you from the House of Hashem. Hashem is God, He has made it light for us; bring the festival offering, bound with cords, to the corners of the altar. Hashem is God, He has made it light for us; bring the festival offering, bound with cords, to the corners of the Altar. You are my God, and I will thank You; my God, and I will exalt You. You are my God, and I will thank You; my God, and I will exalt You. Give thanks to Hashem, for He is good; His kindness endures forever. Give thanks to Hashem, for He is good; His kindness endures forever.

All Your creations shall praise You, Hashem, our God. Your devout ones, the righteous who do Your will, and Your entire nation the House of Israel, with great joy will thank, bless, praise, glorify, exalt, extol, sanctify, and announce the majesty of Your Name, our King. For to You it is good to give thanks, and to Your Name it is pleasant to sing. In this world and for eternity You are God.

כִּי לְעוֹלָם חַסְדּוֹ	הוֹדוּ לַיְיָ כִּי טוֹב
כִּי לְעוֹלָם חַסְדּוֹ	הוֹדוּ לֵאלֹהֵי הָאֱלֹהִים
כִּי לְעוֹלָם חַסְדּוֹ	הוֹדוּ לַאֲדֹנֵי הָאֲדֹנִים
כִּי לְעוֹלָם חַסְדּוֹ	לְעֹשֵׂה נִפְלָאוֹת גְּדֹלוֹת לְבַדּוֹ
כִּי לְעוֹלָם חַסְדּוֹ	לְעֹשֵׂה הַשָּׁמַיִם בִּתְבוּנָה
כִּי לְעוֹלָם חַסְדּוֹ	לְרוֹקַע הָאָרֶץ עַל הַמָּיִם
כִּי לְעוֹלָם חַסְדּוֹ	לְעֹשֵׂה אוֹרִים גְּדֹלִים
כִּי לְעוֹלָם חַסְדּוֹ	אֶת הַשֶּׁמֶשׁ לְמֶמְשֶׁלֶת בַּיּוֹם
כִּי לְעוֹלָם חַסְדּוֹ	אֶת הַיָּרֵחַ וְכוֹכָבִים לְמֶמְשְׁלוֹת בַּלָּיְלָה
כִּי לְעוֹלָם חַסְדּוֹ	לְמַכֵּה מִצְרַיִם בִּבְכוֹרֵיהֶם
כִּי לְעוֹלָם חַסְדּוֹ	וַיּוֹצֵא יִשְׂרָאֵל מִתּוֹכָם
כִּי לְעוֹלָם חַסְדּוֹ	בְּיָד חֲזָקָה וּבִזְרוֹעַ נְטוּיָה
כִּי לְעוֹלָם חַסְדּוֹ	לְגֹזֵר יַם סוּף לִגְזָרִים

The sun to rule by day

אֶת הַשֶּׁמֶשׁ לְמֶמְשֶׁלֶת בַּיּוֹם

We Jewish people have a calendar that depends on the moon. The whole world thinks the sun is more important, but we say the moon is more important. The holy Zohar says, "The sun reflects the outside light of God, but the moon is the inside." The Jewish nation are the moon people. All the nations count by the sun: they are all of them the surface of the world. But the Jewish nation, the moon nation, is the inside, the soul.

Let's say, I love someone. So you know what we do? We go out at exactly twelve o'clock and look at the sun. How does that sound? It sound crazy, you say. But tell me, why not? Because the sun doesn't show you anything which is deep; it only shows you the skin. Why do business meetings take place during the day? When people are doing business they can't stand the moon: it shows too much. When you love somebody very much, you want to meet them when the moon is shining at night. During the day I can meet with people I can't stand, but at night, never.

Give thanks to Hashem for He is good, for His kindness endures forever.

Give thanks to the God of Gods, for His kindness endures forever.

Give thanks to the Master of Masters, for His kindness endures forever.

To Him Who alone does great wonders, for His kindness endures forever.

To Him Who made the heavens with understanding, for His kindness endures forever.

To Him Who spread out the earth upon the water, for His kindness endures forever.

To Him Who made great lights, for His kindness endures forever.

The sun to rule by day, for His kindness endures forever.

The moon and the stars to rule by night, for His kindness endures forever.

To Him Who smote Egypt through their firstborn, for His kindness endures forever.

And brought Israel out from their midst, for His kindness endures forever.

With a mighty hand and an outstretched arm, for His kindness endures forever.

To Him Who divided the Red Sea, for His kindness endures forever.

כִּי לְעוֹלָם חַסְדּוֹ	וְהֶעֱבִיר יִשְׂרָאֵל בְּתוֹכוֹ
כִּי לְעוֹלָם חַסְדּוֹ	וְנִעֵר פַּרְעֹה וְחֵילוֹ בְיַם סוּף
כִּי לְעוֹלָם חַסְדּוֹ	לְמוֹלִיךְ עַמּוֹ בַּמִּדְבָּר
כִּי לְעוֹלָם חַסְדּוֹ	לְמַכֵּה מְלָכִים גְּדֹלִים
כִּי לְעוֹלָם חַסְדּוֹ	וַיַּהֲרֹג מְלָכִים אַדִּירִים
כִּי לְעוֹלָם חַסְדּוֹ	לְסִיחוֹן מֶלֶךְ הָאֱמֹרִי
כִּי לְעוֹלָם חַסְדּוֹ	וּלְעוֹג מֶלֶךְ הַבָּשָׁן
כִּי לְעוֹלָם חַסְדּוֹ	וְנָתַן אַרְצָם לְנַחֲלָה
כִּי לְעוֹלָם חַסְדּוֹ	נַחֲלָה לְיִשְׂרָאֵל עַבְדּוֹ
כִּי לְעוֹלָם חַסְדּוֹ	שֶׁבְּשִׁפְלֵנוּ זָכַר לָנוּ
כִּי לְעוֹלָם חַסְדּוֹ	וַיִּפְרְקֵנוּ מִצָּרֵינוּ
כִּי לְעוֹלָם חַסְדּוֹ	נֹתֵן לֶחֶם לְכָל בָּשָׂר
כִּי לְעוֹלָם חַסְדּוֹ	הוֹדוּ לְאֵל הַשָּׁמָיִם

According to our tradition, even among the Jewish people there are sun people and moon people. Sun people sleep all night, or go out and have a shallow "good time." The moon people among us are up all night doing deeper things. Perhaps they're getting in touch with God, or enriching their souls. The moon people know the light of the night is so much deeper.

The moon came before God and said, "There are two kings here that have the same power. It won't work." So God said to the moon, "Okay, then you make yourself smaller." The way the world, the sun people, understand it, God punished the moon for having the chutzpah to question His will. God created you this way, so stick to it. But the real people say, "The moon was right: there can't be two cooks in the kitchen. Even less can there be two

And led Israel through it, for His kindness endures forever.

And shook Pharaoh and his army into the Red Sea, for His kindness endures forever.

To Him who led His people through the wilderness, for His kindness endures forever.

To Him Who smote great kings, for His kindness endures forever.

And killed mighty kings, for His kindness endures forever.

Sichon king of the Emorites, for His kindness endures forever.

And Og king of Bashan, for His kindness endures forever.

And gave us their land as a heritage, for His kindness endures forever.

A heritage for Israel His servant, for His kindness endures forever.

For in our lowliness He remembered us, for His kindness endures forever.

And released us from our tormentors, for His kindness endures forever.

He gives bread to all flesh, for His kindness endures forever.

Give thanks to God of the heavens, for His kindness endures forever.

lights in the world."

Open your hearts — here is a Torah from Rebbe Nachman: The moon was saying to God, "Is this all the light You can give the world? The light of the sun, which shows only the outside? Isn't there a deeper light available?" God said, "You're the one who will receive this light."

The outside people are always the same: like the sun, they either shine or they're dark. Either they love you or they hate you — so stupid and meaningless. The moon people change all the time: one time I'm full, another time I am a crescent, and sometimes I don't shine at all. Because the more real something is, the more I have to make a separate decision about it every second.

I had a great Rabbi, my teacher, who said to me, "If you ever want to be anything in the world, it has to be clear to you that whatever you knew yesterday is meaningless today." I'm sure it's clear to you that God is not a *yenta*, a chatterbox who says the same things all day long. God can't stand the same thing twice. The sun is always the same; the moon is different every day. Each day a new light comes down from heaven, every day God wants different things from us.

When the Strelisker Rebbe passed away, his children came before the Rhiziner Rebbe. He asked them, "What was the most important thing to your father?" They said to him, "To him, what to do right now was most important." Most people have the general idea: life is all planned out for them forever. But when it comes to the moment they have no idea what to do.

We have to be in tune with the moment. You can be the greatest scholar in the world and not know what to do now. Sometimes a person asks you a question, but what he asks isn't what he really wants. What he needs right now you'll never know. He doesn't know himself. It's so deep to know what you're supposed to do at this moment, to be in touch with the moment. And I don't mean that you have a paperback book titled *What To Do Right Now*.

You know what it is: people say, "I have my principles." But do you know what the greatest principle in the world is? Not to have principles. There's no justice in the world because of all the principles. A poor, starving man comes to the office, and I tell him, "Sorry, we can't help you. It's the weekend and we're closed until Monday."

The sun's light is so big. For us, though, the month begins with just a little ray of moonlight. You know what's going on here? From themselves people expect nothing. But when it comes to others — if they don't shine like the sun they don't count. It has to be the other way around: from myself I have to ask everything; from somebody else, one little ray of light and I'm so proud of him.

Imagine if, in the schools, instead of giving marks when you're bad they gave marks for every ray of light. Suppose a moon teacher has a boy or girl that's really having a hard time in school; it takes so much out of them just to do the little they are doing. I'd say to them, "Every little ray of light means more to me than the light of the sun." You never know: some people can run ten thousand miles, and others have trouble taking even one step.

One more thing which is very important: sun people are full of themselves — so proud, so arrogant. The moment the moon is full he says to God, "I can't stand myself any more. I'm full of me. Master of the world, give me a deeper light."

According to our tradition, the moon of this month is not the same as last month's moon. It's new. Seven days after the new moon we go out and greet this month's moon. It's a custom that we do it together with our friends, and then we greet each other with *Shalom Aleichem*. What's the first sign that a person is new? When everybody else looks new to him. You're so beautiful, he thinks; how come I never noticed? The moon doesn't take away the darkness: it's still dark, but there's also light.

I want to share something deep with you. You have friends, sun friends, and when they start asking you questions, they squeeze out every bit of information that you'd like to keep private. The sun people kill each other. The moon people, for every ray of light, every bit of information, say, "Thank you so much."

A secret, according to Kabbalistic tradition, is not something you don't know and I do know, something that I can tell you. That's not a secret, just a thing you didn't know and now you do know. A secret is something that, even after I know, I still don't know.

Why do we say every day that God is One? Hashem should tell us, "You're getting on my nerves." Let's put it this way: I love my wife very much. At two-thirty I tell her, "I love you so much." At two-forty, "I love you so much." Then at three o'clock I tell her the same thing again. There are two reactions: if my wife is a sun woman, she thinks, "he told me at two-thirty, right, then he told me again at two-forty." She says, "Enough. You just told me that." How does it sound to you?

The other side: if my wife is a moon woman, when I tell her at two-forty she asks, "Why did you wait ten minutes to tell me again?" Because she knows that every time I say it, it gets deeper and deeper. There's no such thing as having told her before.

It's such a great privilege to love somebody very much. If I love you, it's clear to me that I don't know all about you, but even the little that I know is enough. Who dares say, "I know you"? At a wedding, when you cover the bride's face you're telling her, "The beginning of all relationships is that it's clear to me that I don't know you. I hope that every day God will reveal to me how little I know you." When I see a father and mother say, "I know my child," I'm ready to adopt the poor kid. Sun people can't bring peace to the world. They say, "I know everything about you. Even though you're bad, we'll make peace." It doesn't go this way. You have to say, "The little I know about you, maybe it's bad, but who knows how much you have there which I don't know yet." That's why after we bless the moon we walk around saying, "Greetings to you, peace to you." Thank You for the inside light.

There are two books in Heaven, the Book of Life and the Book of Death, and every person is inscribed in one of them. When God inscribes someone in the Book of Death, God forbid, that's when you are shallow, involved only in the exterior — it means you're being nothing. The Book of Life is inside, way inside.

Every new friendship can be written in the Book of Life or the Book of Death. Sometimes we see single people: they meet each other, ask each other, "What do you do? Where do you live? How much money do you make?" — all those sun questions. Sometimes moon people are privileged to meet each other, and then it's so deep.

The Torah is written on parchment. The letters occupy very little space; the empty parchment is so deep.

There were two great Kabbalists who corresponded for years. One would write, "To my holy friend Avraham" and leave the rest of the letter blank, and put at the bottom, "signed, Baruch." The other would write the same way: "To my holy friend Baruch," and then blank paper and at the bottom, "signed, Avraham." They corresponded for ten years. Someone said to one of them, "What kind of correspondence is this?" He said, "When you write with your hands, you have to put in a lot of words. When you write with your soul, you can just send empty space." May God bless us all to have different eyes: not to see what is, but to see that which we cannot see.

He gives bread to all flesh   נותן לחם לכל בשר

The *heilige* Rebbe Elimelech one time was very sick; for days he couldn't eat. His son Rebbe Eliezer came to his father and was pleading with him to eat. This is what Rebbe Elimelech said to him: "Believe me, there is only one thing I'd like to eat: the soup made by Chanele the wife of Avremele the water carrier." So Rebbe Eliezer went to the broken-down house of Avremele the water carrier, knocked on the door, and said, "Chanele, tell me, what kind of soup did you give my holy father?"

Her eyes filled with tears and she said, "I'm ashamed to say it wasn't real soup; it was just ordinary hot water. The *heilige* Rebbe Elimelech came to visit my husband, and it was so beautiful, so heavenly; it was *mamash Gan Eden*. But suddenly my husband said, 'Chanele, bring something to eat for the great guest.' I went into the kitchen, and only then I realized that my husband and I hadn't eaten for three days. Because of Rebbe Elimelech, I completely forgot that we were so hungry.

"I had nothing in the house to give the Rebbe to eat. The only thing I saw was a little water boiling on the stove. I took a spoon, stirred the water, and this is what I said: '*Ribbono Shel Olam, Tatte zisse,* my sweet Father, I'm Chanele, the wife of Avremele. I have nothing in the house to give the holy Rebbe. But *Tatte zisse,* You have *Gan Eden,* You have everything. I'm crying before You, put a little bit of *Gan Eden* in this hot water so Rebbe Elimelech can taste something good.'"

Rebbe Eliezer went back to his father and said, "Regards from Chanele." The *heilige* Rebbe Elimelech was smiling, and he said, "Eliezer, don't you understand, there's soup that you feed the hungry people of the world, but Chanele's soup can be *mechayeh meisim;* it has the power to bring people back to life."

So this is what I, Shlomo ben Pesia, wish to all of the mothers and fathers in the world. Sometimes our children come home and all they need is some ordinary soup. But sometimes their *neshamos* are hungry for the soup of Chanele, the wife of the *heilige* Avremele, the water carrier.

נִשְׁמַת כָּל חַי תְּבָרֵךְ אֶת שִׁמְךָ יְיָ אֱלֹהֵינוּ וְרוּחַ כָּל בָּשָׂר
תְּפָאֵר וּתְרוֹמֵם זִכְרְךָ מַלְכֵּנוּ תָּמִיד מִן הָעוֹלָם וְעַד הָעוֹלָם
אַתָּה אֵל וּמִבַּלְעָדֶיךָ אֵין לָנוּ מֶלֶךְ גּוֹאֵל וּמוֹשִׁיעַ פּוֹדֶה
וּמַצִּיל וּמְפַרְנֵס וּמְרַחֵם בְּכָל עֵת צָרָה וְצוּקָה אֵין לָנוּ מֶלֶךְ
אֶלָּא אָתָּה. אֱלֹהֵי הָרִאשׁוֹנִים וְהָאַחֲרוֹנִים. אֱלוֹהַּ כָּל בְּרִיּוֹת
אֲדוֹן כָּל תּוֹלָדוֹת הַמְהֻלָּל (בְּכָל) בְּרוֹב הַתִּשְׁבָּחוֹת הַמְנַהֵג
עוֹלָמוֹ בְּחֶסֶד וּבְרִיּוֹתָיו בְּרַחֲמִים. וַיְיָ עֵר הִנֵּה לֹא יָנוּם וְלֹא
יִישָׁן. הַמְּעוֹרֵר יְשֵׁנִים וְהַמֵּקִיץ נִרְדָּמִים (מְחַיֶּה מֵתִים וְרוֹפֵא
חוֹלִים, פּוֹקֵחַ עִוְרִים וְזוֹקֵף כְּפוּפִים) הַמֵּשִׂיחַ אִלְּמִים וְהַמַּתִּיר
אֲסוּרִים וְהַסּוֹמֵךְ נוֹפְלִים וְהַזּוֹקֵף כְּפוּפִים וְהַמְפַעֲנֵחַ נֶעְלָמִים.
לְךָ לְבַדְּךָ אֲנַחְנוּ מוֹדִים. וְאִלּוּ פִינוּ מָלֵא שִׁירָה כַּיָּם וּלְשׁוֹנֵנוּ
רִנָּה כַּהֲמוֹן גַּלָּיו וְשִׂפְתוֹתֵינוּ שֶׁבַח כְּמֶרְחֲבֵי רָקִיעַ וְעֵינֵינוּ
מְאִירוֹת כַּשֶּׁמֶשׁ וְכַיָּרֵחַ וְיָדֵינוּ פְרוּשׂוֹת כְּנִשְׁרֵי שָׁמָיִם וְרַגְלֵינוּ
קַלּוֹת כָּאַיָּלוֹת אֵין אֲנַחְנוּ מַסְפִּיקִים לְהוֹדוֹת לְךָ יְיָ אֱלֹהֵינוּ
וֵאלֹהֵי אֲבוֹתֵינוּ וּלְבָרֵךְ אֶת שִׁמְךָ עַל אַחַת מֵאֶלֶף אֶלֶף
אַלְפֵי אֲלָפִים וְרִבֵּי רְבָבוֹת פְּעָמִים הַטּוֹבוֹת נִסִּים וְנִפְלָאוֹת
שֶׁעָשִׂיתָ עִם אֲבוֹתֵינוּ וְעִמָּנוּ. מִלְּפָנִים מִמִּצְרַיִם גְּאַלְתָּנוּ יְיָ
אֱלֹהֵינוּ וּמִבֵּית עֲבָדִים פְּדִיתָנוּ. בְּרָעָב זַנְתָּנוּ. וּבְשָׂבָע
כִּלְכַּלְתָּנוּ. מֵחֶרֶב הִצַּלְתָּנוּ. וּמִדֶּבֶר מִלַּטְתָּנוּ. וּמֵחֳלָיִם רָעִים
וְרַבִּים וְנֶאֱמָנִים דִּלִּיתָנוּ. עַד הֵנָּה עֲזָרוּנוּ רַחֲמֶיךָ. וְלֹא עֲזָבוּנוּ
חֲסָדֶיךָ יְיָ אֱלֹהֵינוּ. וְאַל תִּטְּשֵׁנוּ יְיָ אֱלֹהֵינוּ לָנֶצַח. עַל כֵּן
אֵבָרִים שֶׁפִּלַּגְתָּ בָּנוּ וְרוּחַ וּנְשָׁמָה שֶׁנָּפַחְתָּ בְּאַפֵּינוּ. וְלָשׁוֹן
אֲשֶׁר שַׂמְתָּ בְּפִינוּ. הֵן הֵם יוֹדוּ וִיבָרְכוּ וִישַׁבְּחוּ וִיפָאֲרוּ
וִישׁוֹרְרוּ וִירוֹמְמוּ וְיַעֲרִיצוּ וְיַקְדִּישׁוּ וְיַמְלִיכוּ אֶת שִׁמְךָ מַלְכֵּנוּ
תָּמִיד. כִּי כָל פֶּה לְךָ יוֹדֶה וְכָל לָשׁוֹן לְךָ תִשָּׁבַע וְכָל עַיִן לְךָ
תְצַפֶּה וְכָל בֶּרֶךְ לְךָ תִכְרַע וְכָל קוֹמָה לְפָנֶיךָ תִשְׁתַּחֲוֶה וְכָל
הַלְּבָבוֹת יִירָאוּךָ וְכָל קֶרֶב וּכְלָיוֹת יְזַמְּרוּ לִשְׁמֶךָ. כַּדָּבָר
שֶׁכָּתוּב כָּל עַצְמוֹתַי תֹּאמַרְנָה יְיָ מִי כָמוֹךָ. מַצִּיל עָנִי מֵחָזָק
מִמֶּנּוּ וְעָנִי וְאֶבְיוֹן מִגֹּזְלוֹ שׁוֹעַת עֲנִיִּים אַתָּה תִשְׁמַע צַעֲקַת

The soul of every living being will bless Your Name.
Hashem our God; the spirit of all flesh will always
glorify and exalt Your remembrance, our King. In this
world and for eternity You are God, and besides You
we have no king, redeemer or savior, who liberates,
rescues, sustains, and has compassion in every time of
trouble and distress – we have no king but You! God
of the first and of the last, God of all creatures, Master of all generations, Who is praised with a multitude
of praises, Who guides His world with kindness and
His creatures with mercy. Hashem neither slumbers
nor sleeps, He Who wakens the sleepers and rouses
the slumberers, Who gives speech to the mute and
releases the bound, Who supports the falling and
straightens the bent. To You and to You alone we
give thanks.

Were our mouths as full of song as the sea, and our
tongue full of ecstasy like its multitude of waves, and
our lips full of praise as the breadth of the heavens,
our eyes as brilliant as the sun and the moon, our
hands spread out like eagles in the sky and our feet as
swift as deer, we still could not thank You enough,
Hashem our God and God of our fathers, or bless
Your Name for even one of the thousand thousands
and myriads of favors that You did for our ancestors
and for us. You redeemed us, Hashem our God, from
Egypt and liberated us from the house of bondage.

הַדַּל תַּקְשִׁיב וְתוֹשִׁיעַ. מִי יִדְמֶה לָּךְ וּמִי יִשְׁוֶה לָּךְ וּמִי יַעֲרָךְ לָךְ הָאֵל הַגָּדוֹל הַגִּבּוֹר וְהַנּוֹרָא אֵל עֶלְיוֹן קוֹנֵה שָׁמַיִם וָאָרֶץ. נְהַלֶּלְךָ וּנְשַׁבֵּחֲךָ וּנְפָאֶרְךָ וּנְבָרֵךְ אֶת שֵׁם קָדְשֶׁךָ. כָּאָמוּר, לְדָוִד, בָּרְכִי נַפְשִׁי אֶת יְיָ וְכָל קְרָבַי אֶת שֵׁם קָדְשׁוֹ:

נשמת כל חי   The soul of every living thing

"*Nishmas kol chai tevareich es shimcha,* the soul of everything alive blesses Your name." The truth is, as long as we're alive — and hopefully we'll be alive forever — we don't stop praying. Each time we take a breath it's the deepest prayer before the One, the Only One.

There's another level, though. I would like, one time in my life, to pour out my heart in the deepest way before the Only One. You know, my dearest friends, at a business meeting we discuss what we need to discuss and we say to each other everything there is to say. But when I meet somebody I love very much, even all of eternity wouldn't be enough to tell them how much I love them and how much I miss them every second of my life.

There is a story about two holy masters: Rebbe Mendele Vitebsker and the holy Kaliszer Rebbe. They went to the Holy Land, to the land of all holiness. The Kaliszer moved to Tzfat and Rebbe Mendele settled in Teveriah. The Kaliszer wrote a letter to the holy Vitebsker, and this is what he wrote: "To my holy friend Rebbe Mendele, may your light shine forever:

"Until I came to the Holy Land my mind was so small! I asked of God each time I prayed, three times a day, that my prayer should be with all my heart. Now that I'm in the Holy Land I understand things so much more deeply, and the truth is shining into my heart. I know that such prayer is beyond me, far beyond me. Now all I'm asking of God is, 'Don't make me leave this world yet; please don't let me leave before I have prayed just one prayer.'"

Rebbe Mendele wrote back to him: "You touched me so deeply with your words that I know you can ask God for one prayer. As for me, though, I'm not even on that level. I'm not asking God even for one prayer. All I'm asking is, 'Let me say just one *word* of prayer before You. Don't let me leave this world without praying one word to You. Let me pour out my heart before You in a single word.'"

In famine You nourished us and in plenty You supported us. From the sword You rescued us; from plague You saved us; and from severe and unending diseases You relieved us. Until now Your mercy has helped us, and Your kindness has not forsaken us; do not, then, abandon us, Hashem our God, forever.

Therefore the limbs that You set out in us, and the spirit and soul which You breathed into our nostrils, and the tongue that You placed in our mouth will all thank, bless, praise, glorify, exalt, extol, sanctify and announce the majesty of Your Name, our King. For every mouth will offer thanks to You; every tongue will swear obedience to You; every knee will bend to You; every upright form will bow down before You; all hearts will revere You, and all innards and thoughts will sing praise to Your name, as it is written: "All my bones shall say: 'Hashem, who is like You?'"

Who is equal to You? Who can be compared to You? Great, mighty, and awesome God, the supreme God, Owner of heaven and earth. We will praise, extol, and glorify You and bless Your holy Name, as it is said, "A song of David: My soul, bless Hashem, and let all my innards bless His holy Name!"

מחליים רעים ונאמנים   From severe and unending diseases

In Viletnik, somewhere in Russia, the *heilige* R. Yisrael was the Rebbe.

In those days all the *Yidden* lived in great peace, in holiness, in sweetness. One day they told the Rebbe that the wife of one of his Chassidim had moved back in with her parents. So he called the lady to come before him and asked her, "Tell me the truth, why did you move back to your parents? I want you to know, your husband is up all night in the *Beis Midrash,* crying and begging God that you should come back."

This is what she said: "*Heilige* Rebbe, my holy master, I want you to know that I didn't leave my husband because I don't love him. On the contrary, we love each other very much. But we have no children, and I can't bear the emptiness in the house any more. A house without the crying of children, without the laughter of babies, is like a burnt Holy Temple, and I just couldn't bear it any more."

Then an idea came to her, and she said, "Rebbe, if you want me to go back to him, bless me to have children." She was a clever woman; right away she added, "As long as you're blessing me, Rebbe, why don't you bless me to have children like you?"

The Rebbe thought for a while, and this is what he said: "If you promise me to be like my mother, I promise you, you'll have children like me.

"Let me tell you a story about my mother. It should never happen to anyone — my father left this world when I was very young, just four years old. My brother was seven. One morning my mother woke up, and she was really sick. She said to me, 'Yisraelik, my precious child, I'm asking you, bring me my prayer book, *der kleiner siddur.* I can't get out of bed, and I have to *daven.'* I brought my mother her *siddur.* She held it in her hands and said, '*Ribbono shel Olam,* Master of the world, I'm so sick I don't even have the strength to pray. But,' she said, 'You know the truth: if I don't take care of my children, nobody else will. So please, for the sake of my children, make me well.' And I tell you," said the Rebbe, "she got out of bed cured."

וכל הלבבות ייראוך   All hearts will revere you

You know, my friends, I'm sure it's clear to you that everyone has his own definition of being holy. But if you don't hear someone's crying you're not holy! Maybe the rest of you is holy, but your ears definitely aren't. We *Yidden* got our holiness from *Shema Yisrael,* by being able to hear Hashem's voice that came all the way from Heaven; the same way, we can hear any cry from however far away it comes.

One Thursday night the holy Baal Shem Tov said, "Harness the horses, we have to go somewhere for Shabbos." But he didn't say where they needed to go. So they travelled all night, just letting the horses lead them, until the horses walked up to a tumbledown hut that sat next to a mansion. A man walked out of it — he looked like a gangster, gruesome like a murderer. He yelled, "What do you want?" The Baal Shem Tov answered softly, with great respect, "May we stay here for Shabbos?" The man answered, "I know people like you; you pray for ten hours, and it takes you forever to make *Kiddush*. I pray for just two minutes and make *Kiddush* in one minute! If you want to stay here, you'll have to do as I do."

The Baal Shem Tov went through Shabbos like that: *davening* in such a rush it didn't even feel like *davening, Kiddush* so fast it was as if no one had made it at all. This Shabbos was more like Tish'ah B'av than Shabbos, not to mention the curses and abuse that the cutthroat of a householder rained on them. But through it all the Baal Shem Tov kept quiet.

After *Havdalah* the gangster disappeared, and suddenly the most elegant lady walked in from the big house next door. She looked like our four Mothers, so holy and beautiful. She said to the Baal Shem Tov, "Holy master, let me have the honor of inviting you to the fourth meal, the 'feast of King David.'" — The Chassidim were stunned; what was going on? — The lady went on, "*Heilige zisse Rebbe,* don't you recognize me?" The Baal Shem Tov looked at her and cried out, "Aren't you Feigele, little Feigele, the orphan girl that worked in our kitchen when you were only nine years old?"

With tears in her eyes Feigele said, "Yes! You remember that I was an orphan, Rebbe; I had no one in the world until you took me in. Do you also remember when I got lice in my head, the way children do? Your Rebbetzin combed them out of my hair — but she did it so roughly that I was crying with the pain. With all my heart I cried out, 'Rebbetzin, please, more gently, I can't bear the pain.' But she wouldn't listen. And you, Rebbe, heard me crying, and you didn't say a word. Your wife would have listened to you, but you didn't stand up for me." The Baal Shem was struck dumb with remorse.

Then Feigele continued, "Shortly after I left your house, I met my holy husband." At that moment the door opened and in walked the "murderer," the "gangster." His face had softened and glowed with light — it was plain to see now that he was the holiest of the holy. Feigele spoke in a whisper: "When I married, my husband said to me, 'You need to know that because of you the *heilige* Baal Shem Tov has no share in the World to Come. When you were crying and the Baal Shem Tov was silent, a voice went out in Heaven that he had lost his share in the World to Come.' I was so sad, Rebbe, because you were so dear to me, my only protector in my childhood; I didn't want you to lose anything on account of me. So my husband took it upon himself to get you back your share in the World to Come. So my husband made one Shabbos of your life into a day of suffering. Now you have atoned, and your share in the World to Come is returned to you."

הָאֵל בְּתַעֲצֻמוֹת עֻזֶּךָ הַגָּדוֹל בִּכְבוֹד שְׁמֶךָ הַגִּבּוֹר לָנֶצַח וְהַנּוֹרָא בְּנוֹרְאוֹתֶיךָ. הַמֶּלֶךְ הַיּוֹשֵׁב עַל כִּסֵּא רָם וְנִשָּׂא:

שׁוֹכֵן עַד מָרוֹם וְקָדוֹשׁ שְׁמוֹ. וְכָתוּב רַנְּנוּ צַדִּיקִים בַּיְיָ לַיְשָׁרִים נָאוָה תְהִלָּה: בְּפִי יְשָׁרִים תִּתְהַלָּל וּבְדִבְרֵי צַדִּיקִים תִּתְבָּרַךְ וּבִלְשׁוֹן חֲסִידִים תִּתְרוֹמָם וּבְקֶרֶב קְדוֹשִׁים תִּתְקַדָּשׁ:

וּבְמַקְהֲלוֹת רִבְבוֹת עַמְּךָ בֵּית יִשְׂרָאֵל בְּרִנָּה יִתְפָּאֵר שִׁמְךָ מַלְכֵּנוּ בְּכָל דּוֹר וָדוֹר שֶׁכֵּן חוֹבַת כָּל הַיְצוּרִים לְפָנֶיךָ יְיָ אֱלֹהֵינוּ וֵאלֹהֵי אֲבוֹתֵינוּ לְהוֹדוֹת לְהַלֵּל לְשַׁבֵּחַ לְפָאֵר לְרוֹמֵם לְהַדֵּר לְבָרֵךְ לְעַלֵּה וּלְקַלֵּס עַל כָּל דִּבְרֵי שִׁירוֹת וְתִשְׁבְּחוֹת דָּוִד בֶּן יִשַׁי עַבְדְּךָ מְשִׁיחֶךָ:

יִשְׁתַּבַּח שִׁמְךָ לָעַד מַלְכֵּנוּ, הָאֵל, הַמֶּלֶךְ הַגָּדוֹל, וְהַקָּדוֹשׁ, בַּשָּׁמַיִם וּבָאָרֶץ. כִּי לְךָ נָאֶה יְיָ אֱלֹהֵינוּ וֵאלֹהֵי אֲבוֹתֵינוּ לְעוֹלָם וָעֶד. שִׁיר וּשְׁבָחָה הַלֵּל וְזִמְרָה עֹז וּמֶמְשָׁלָה נֶצַח גְּדֻלָּה וּגְבוּרָה תְּהִלָּה וְתִפְאֶרֶת קְדֻשָּׁה וּמַלְכוּת. בְּרָכוֹת וְהוֹדָאוֹת מֵעַתָּה וְעַד עוֹלָם:

שיר ושבחה · **Song and praise**

There's a Torah thought from Rebbe Nachman: Why is it that when someone talks, the more you look at him while he's talking the more you can understand what he is saying? But when someone is singing, when you close your eyes you hear the *niggun* better. Another thing: why is it that when someone is talking, *trei kali lo mishtam'i*, you can't hear two people's voices at once? But with *neginah*, singing, the more people sing together the more beautiful it is.

O God, in the abundance of Your strength, great in the glory of Your Name, mighty forever and awesome through Your awesome deeds, the King who sits upon a high and lofty throne, He Who is forever, exalted and holy is His Name! And it is written: "Exult, righteous ones, before Hashem; for the upright praise is fitting." By the mouth of the upright You are praised; with the words of the righteous You are blessed; by the tongue of the devout You are exalted; and in the midst of the holy ones You are sanctified. And in the assembled multitudes of Your people, the House of Israel, with joyous song Your Name is glorified, our King, in every generation. For such is the duty of all creatures before You, Hashem our God, God of our fathers, to thank, praise, glorify, exalt, honor, bless, extol, and celebrate, even after all the songs and praises of David ben Yishai, Your anointed servant.

May Your Name be praised forever, our King, the God and King Who is great and holy in heaven and on earth. Because for You are fitting, Hashem our God and the God of our fathers, song and praise, laud and hymns, strength and dominion, victory, greatness and power, praise and splendor, holiness and kingship, blessings and thanksgivings from now and forever.

Rebbe Nachman says, words are on the level of the *asarah ma'amaros*, the Ten Pronouncements the world was created with. Therefore, when someone talks he's using worldly tools. Singing, however, comes from the world which is beyond Creation. If I sing one thing and you sing something

בָּרוּךְ אַתָּה יְיָ אֵל מֶלֶךְ גָּדוֹל וּמְהֻלָּל בַּתִּשְׁבָּחוֹת. אֵל הַהוֹדָאוֹת, אֲדוֹן הַנִּפְלָאוֹת, הַבּוֹחֵר בְּשִׁירֵי זִמְרָה, מֶלֶךְ אֵל, חֵי הָעוֹלָמִים:

The fourth cup is drunk while reclining to the left side.

בָּרוּךְ אַתָּה יְיָ אֱלֹהֵינוּ מֶלֶךְ הָעוֹלָם בּוֹרֵא פְּרִי הַגָּפֶן:

After drinking the fourth cup the concluding blessing is recited. On Shabbos include the passage in parentheses.

בָּרוּךְ אַתָּה יְיָ אֱלֹהֵינוּ מֶלֶךְ הָעוֹלָם עַל הַגֶּפֶן וְעַל פְּרִי הַגֶּפֶן וְעַל תְּנוּבַת הַשָּׂדֶה וְעַל אֶרֶץ חֶמְדָּה טוֹבָה וּרְחָבָה שֶׁרָצִיתָ וְהִנְחַלְתָּ לַאֲבוֹתֵינוּ לֶאֱכוֹל מִפִּרְיָהּ וְלִשְׂבּוֹעַ מִטּוּבָהּ. רַחֵם (נָא) יְיָ אֱלֹהֵינוּ עַל יִשְׂרָאֵל עַמֶּךָ וְעַל יְרוּשָׁלַיִם עִירֶךָ וְעַל צִיּוֹן מִשְׁכַּן כְּבוֹדֶךָ וְעַל מִזְבְּחֶךָ וְעַל הֵיכָלֶךָ וּבְנֵה יְרוּשָׁלַיִם עִיר הַקֹּדֶשׁ בִּמְהֵרָה בְיָמֵינוּ וְהַעֲלֵנוּ לְתוֹכָהּ וְשַׂמְּחֵנוּ בְּבִנְיָנָהּ וְנֹאכַל מִפִּרְיָהּ וְנִשְׂבַּע מִטּוּבָהּ וּנְבָרֶכְךָ עָלֶיהָ בִּקְדֻשָּׁה וּבְטָהֳרָה (בשבת: וּרְצֵה וְהַחֲלִיצֵנוּ בְּיוֹם הַשַּׁבָּת הַזֶּה). וְשַׂמְּחֵנוּ בְּיוֹם חַג הַמַּצּוֹת הַזֶּה. כִּי אַתָּה יְיָ טוֹב וּמֵטִיב לַכֹּל וְנוֹדֶה לְךָ עַל הָאָרֶץ וְעַל פְּרִי הַגָּפֶן. בָּרוּךְ אַתָּה יְיָ עַל הָאָרֶץ וְעַל פְּרִי הַגָּפֶן:

else, it can become harmony.

When someone talks, you look at the person. But when someone is singing, you close your eyes, because singing is so heavenly. The less you're on this world, the less you're looking at the world, the more you know what to sing about.

Blessed are You, Hashem, God, King Who is great in praise, God to Whom all give thanks, Master of wonders, Who is pleased with tuneful songs, King, God, Life of all worlds.

The fourth cup is drunk while reclining to the left side.

Blessed are You, Hashem, our God, King of the universe, Creator of the fruit of the vine.

After drinking the fourth cup the concluding blessing is recited. On Shabbos include the passage in parentheses.

Blessed are You, Hashem, our God, King of the universe, for the vine and the fruit of the vine, and for the produce of the field; and for the desirable, good, and spacious land that You agreed to give our fathers as a heritage, to eat of its fruit and to be satisfied with its goodness. Have mercy, we beg You, Hashem our God, on Israel Your people; on Yerushalayim Your city; on Zion, the resting place of Your glory; and on Your altar and Your Temple. Rebuild Yerushalayim, the city of holiness, speedily in our days. Bring us up into it, and make us happy with its rebuilding, and let us eat of its fruit and be satisfied with its goodness, and bless You for it in holiness and purity. (And liberate us with good will on this Shabbos day,) and make us happy on this day of the Festival of Matzos; for You, Hashem, are good and continually do good to all, and we thank You for the land and for the fruit of the vine. Blessed are You, Hashem, for the land and for the fruit of the vine.

נִרְצָה

חֲסַל סִדּוּר פֶּסַח כְּהִלְכָתוֹ. כְּכָל מִשְׁפָּטוֹ וְחֻקָּתוֹ. כַּאֲשֶׁר זָכִינוּ
לְסַדֵּר אוֹתוֹ. כֵּן נִזְכֶּה לַעֲשׂוֹתוֹ. זָךְ שׁוֹכֵן מְעוֹנָה. קוֹמֵם
קְהַל עֲדַת מִי מָנָה. קָרֵב נַהֵל נִטְעֵי כַנָּה. פְּדוּיִם לְצִיּוֹן
בְּרִנָּה:

Some say three times:

לְשָׁנָה הַבָּאָה בִּירוּשָׁלָיִם:

לשנה הבאה בירושלים   **Next year in Yerushalayim**

The Tzanzer Rebbe, a hundred and fifty years ago, had only one good
foot. He could only limp about, but when anyone told him, "I'm going to
Yerushalayim, the holy city," as hard as it was for him, he would not only
walk them to the door, he would walk behind them down the street and say,
"Give my regards to Yerushalayim, to every house, to every tree, every leaf,
every flower, to every cloud, every star. Give my regards to the holy Wall.
Tell Yerushalayim we're coming. It's true that we're limping. We're broken.
We can't walk fast. But we're coming."

When you come to Yerushalayim, your heart is so full, yet so broken. We
were the most heartbroken of all after the gas chambers killed six million. A
million children. But with our hearts broken, we went back to the heartbroken city — the only city that can fill our hearts, the city that's so deep, it
keeps our hearts broken while it's full. It's so full that your heart has to
break, because it's deeper than you can take.

We *Yidden* are infinite. That means we are whole and broken, broken and
whole. When you walk on the street and see a poor man, you give him five
dollars. If you give it to him without being broken because of it, you've just
given him some green paper. But if it breaks your heart, you've given him a
new soul — you make a poor man whole again.

Can you imagine? From Auschwitz straight to Yerushalayim, and we're

Nirtzah

The Seder is ended in accordance with its laws, all of its ordinances and statutes. Just as we were privileged to celebrate it, so may we merit to perform it. Pure One Who dwells on high, restore the congregation that cannot be counted. Soon may You guide the offshoots of Your plants to Zion, redeemed, with song.

Some say three times:

Next year in Yerushalayim

still walking. *L'shanah haba'ah biyerushalayim!*

וּבְכֵן וַיְהִי בַּחֲצִי הַלַּיְלָה

הַלַּיְלָה	וּבְכֵן וַיְהִי בַּחֲצִי
בַּלַּיְלָה	אָז רֹב נִסִּים הִפְלֵאתָ
הַלַּיְלָה	בְּרֹאשׁ אַשְׁמוֹרֶת זֶה
לַיְלָה	גֵּר צֶדֶק נִצַּחְתּוֹ כְּנֶחֱלַק לוֹ
הַלַּיְלָה	וַיְהִי בַּחֲצִי הַלַּיְלָה דַּנְתָּ מֶלֶךְ גְּרָר בַּחֲלוֹם
לַיְלָה	הִפְחַדְתָּ אֲרַמִּי בְּאֶמֶשׁ
לַיְלָה	וַיִּשַּׂר יִשְׂרָאֵל לְמַלְאָךְ וַיּוּכַל לוֹ
הַלַּיְלָה הַלַּיְלָה	וַיְהִי בַּחֲצִי הַלַּיְלָה זֶרַע בְּכוֹרֵי פַתְרוֹס מָחַצְתָּ בַּחֲצִי
בַּלַּיְלָה	חֵילָם לֹא מָצְאוּ בְּקוּמָם
לַיְלָה	טִיסַת נְגִיד חֲרֹשֶׁת סִלִּיתָ בְּכוֹכְבֵי
	וַיְהִי בַּחֲצִי הַלַּיְלָה יָעַץ מְחָרֵף לְנוֹפֵף אִוּוּי
בַּלַּיְלָה	הוֹבַשְׁתָּ פְגָרָיו
לַיְלָה	כָּרַע בֵּל וּמַצָּבוֹ בְּאִישׁוֹן

And it came to pass at midnight!
Then, in times of old, you performed many wonders by night
At the beginning of the watches of this night.
To the righteous convert (Avraham) You gave victory by dividing for him the night.

> It came to pass at midnight.

You judged the king of Gerar (Avimelech) in a dream at night.
You frightened the Aramean (Lavan) in the dark of night.
Yisrael fought an angel and overcame him at night.

> It came to pass at midnight.

You crushed the first-born of Pasros (Egypt) at midnight.
They did not find their host upon arising at night.
The army of the prince of Charoshes (Sisera) You swept away with the stars of the night.

> It came to pass at midnight.

The blasphemer (Sancheirev) planned to raise his hand against Yerushalayim; but You made him into dry corpses in the night.
Bel with its pedestal was overturned in the darkness of night.

לְאִישׁ חֲמוּדוֹת נִגְלָה רָז חֲזוֹת | לַיְלָה

וַיְהִי בַּחֲצִי הַלַּיְלָה מִשְׁתַּכֵּר בִּכְלֵי קֹדֶשׁ נֶהֱרַג בּוֹ | בַּלַּיְלָה

נוֹשַׁע מִבּוֹר אֲרָיוֹת פּוֹתֵר בִּעֲתוּתֵי | לַיְלָה

שִׂנְאָה נָטַר אֲגָגִי וְכָתַב סְפָרִים | בַּלַּיְלָה

וַיְהִי בַּחֲצִי הַלַּיְלָה עוֹרַרְתָּ נִצְחֲךָ עָלָיו בְּנֶדֶד שְׁנַת | לַיְלָה

פּוּרָה תִדְרֹךְ לְשׁוֹמֵר מַה | מִלַּיְלָה

צָרַח כַּשׁוֹמֵר וְשָׂח אָתָא בֹקֶר וְגַם | לַיְלָה

וַיְהִי בַּחֲצִי הַלַּיְלָה קָרֵב יוֹם אֲשֶׁר הוּא לֹא יוֹם וְלֹא | לַיְלָה

רָם הוֹדַע כִּי לְךָ יוֹם אַף לְךָ | לַיְלָה

שׁוֹמְרִים הַפְקֵד לְעִירְךָ כָּל הַיּוֹם וְכָל | הַלַּיְלָה

תָּאִיר כְּאוֹר יוֹם חֶשְׁכַּת | לַיְלָה

וַיְהִי בַּחֲצִי | הַלַּיְלָה

Appoint guards for Your city   שומרים הפקד לעירך

Every second we miss Yerushalayim, but that doesn't compare to how much we miss it on the *shalosh regalim.* On Pesach, Shavuos, and Sukkos, *gevalt* we miss Yerushalayim so much.

Three years ago I was in Russia. I learned thousands of things from the holy *Yidden* in Russia. But one thing I learned from them that no one else can teach me:

Let's say Mashiach comes to us right now and says, "Let's go to Yerushalayim." Everybody would run to a phone, one to cancel an appointment, one to make other arrangements. And someone would say, "Do I have to come right now?" Everyone would have an excuse. In the meantime Mashiach would say, "If you're not ready, I'm going home."

Out of all the people in the world, the people who are the most ready for Mashiach are the Russian Jews. Once a year, on Seder night, we open the door and tell Eliyahu Hanavi, "Please come; I'm ready to go to the holy city of Yerushalayim."

To the man You delighted in (Daniel) was revealed the secret of the visions of night.
It came to pass at midnight.
He who became drunk from the holy vessels (Belshazzar) was killed that very night.
Saved from lion's den was he (Daniel) who interpreted the horrors of the night.
The Aggagi (Haman) nursed hatred and wrote edicts by night.
It came to pass at midnight.
You began Your victory over him with disturbing (Achashveirosh's) sleep at night.
Trample the wine-press for those who ask the watchman, "What will come of the night?"
He will shout, like a watchman, and say: "Morning shall come and also night."
It came to pass at midnight.
Bring close the day (of Mashiach) that is neither day nor night.
Exalted One, make known that Yours is the day and Yours also is the night.
Appoint guards for Your city, all day and all night.
Brighten like the light of day the darkness of night.
It came to pass at midnight.

וַאֲמַרְתֶּם זֶבַח פֶּסַח:

וּבְכֵן וַאֲמַרְתֶּם זֶבַח	פֶּסַח:
אֹמֶץ גְּבוּרוֹתֶיךָ הִפְלֵאתָ	בַּפֶּסַח:
בְּרֹאשׁ כָּל מוֹעֲדוֹת נִשֵּׂאתָ	פֶּסַח:
גִּלִּיתָ לְאֶזְרָחִי חֲצוֹת לֵיל	פֶּסַח:
וַאֲמַרְתֶּם זֶבַח פֶּסַח: דְּלָתָיו דָּפַקְתָּ כְּחֹם הַיּוֹם	בַּפֶּסַח:
הִסְעִיד נוֹצְצִים עֻגוֹת מַצּוֹת	בַּפֶּסַח:
וְאֶל הַבָּקָר רָץ זֵכֶר לְשׁוֹר עֵרֶךְ	פֶּסַח:
וַאֲמַרְתֶּם זֶבַח פֶּסַח: זוֹעֲמוּ סְדוֹמִים וְלוֹהֲטוּ בָּאֵשׁ	בַּפֶּסַח:
חֻלַּץ לוֹט מֵהֶם וּמַצּוֹת אָפָה בְּקֵץ	פֶּסַח:
טֵאטֵאתָ אַדְמַת מוֹף וְנוֹף בְּעָבְרְךָ	בַּפֶּסַח:
וַאֲמַרְתֶּם זֶבַח	פֶּסַח:
יָהּ רֹאשׁ כָּל הוֹן מָחַצְתָּ בְּלֵיל שִׁמּוּר	פֶּסַח:
כַּבִּיר עַל בֵּן בְּכוֹר פָּסַחְתָּ בְּדַם	פֶּסַח:

And you shall say: This is the Passover sacrifice.
You displayed Your mighty powers wondrously on Passover.
Above all seasons of delight You elevated Passover.
You revealed the Exodus to the Oriental (Avraham) at midnight of Passover.

And You shall say: This is the Passover sacrifice.
You knocked at his door in the heat of the day on Passover.
He gave the angels cakes of matzah to dine on during Passover.
He ran to the herd, harbinger of the sacrificial feast of Passover.

And you shall say: This is the Passover sacrifice.
The Sodomites provoked (God) and were burned up with fire on Passover.
Lot was rescued from them and he baked matzos at the end of Passover.
You swept the ground of Moph and Noph (Egypt) when You passed through.

And you shall say: This is the Passover sacrifice.
God, You crushed the head of every firstborn on the watchful night of Passover.
Powerful One, You skipped over Your firstborn by merit of the blood of Passover,

לְבִלְתִּי תֵּת מַשְׁחִית לָבֹא בִּפְתָחָי   בַּפֶּסַח:

וַאֲמַרְתֶּם זֶבַח פֶּסַח: מִסְגֶּרֶת סֻגְּרָה בְּעִתּוֹתֵי   פֶּסַח:

נִשְׁמְדָה מִדְיָן בִּצְלִיל שְׂעוֹרֵי עֹמֶר   פֶּסַח:

שֹׂרְפוּ מִשְׁמַנֵּי פּוּל וְלוּד בִּיקַד יְקוֹד   פֶּסַח:

וַאֲמַרְתֶּם זֶבַח   פֶּסַח:

עוֹד הַיּוֹם בְּנֹב לַעֲמֹד עַד גָּעָה עוֹנַת   פֶּסַח:

פַּס יָד כָּתְבָה לְקַעֲקֵעַ צוּל   בַּפֶּסַח:

צָפֹה הַצָּפִית עָרוֹךְ הַשֻּׁלְחָן   בַּפֶּסַח:

וַאֲמַרְתֶּם זֶבַח   פֶּסַח:

קָהָל כִּנְּסָה הֲדַסָּה צוֹם לְשַׁלֵּשׁ   בַּפֶּסַח:

רֹאשׁ מִבֵּית רָשָׁע מָחַצְתָּ בְּעֵץ חֲמִשִּׁים   בַּפֶּסַח:

שְׁתֵּי אֵלֶּה רֶגַע תָּבִיא לְעוּצִית   בַּפֶּסַח:

תָּעֹז יָדְךָ תָּרוּם יְמִינְךָ כְּלֵיל הִתְקַדֶּשׁ חַג   פֶּסַח:

וַאֲמַרְתֶּם זֶבַח   פֶּסַח:

וַאֲמַרְתֶּם זֶבַח   פֶּסַח:

So as not to let the Destroyer enter my threshold on Passover.

And you shall say: This is the Passover sacrifice.

The besieged city (Jericho) was besieged at the time of Passover.

Midian was destroyed through a barley cake, from the Omer of Passover.

The mighty nobles of Pul and Lud (Assyria) were burnt in a great conflagration on Passover.

And you shall say: This is the Passover sacrifice.

Still today (Sancheirev) would be standing at Nov until the time came for Passover.

A hand inscribed the destruction of Tzul (Babylon) on Passover,

As the watch was set, and the table on Passover.

And you shall say: This is the Passover sacrifice.

Hadassah (Esther) assembled a congregation for a three-day fast on Passover.

The head of the wicked clan (Haman) you crushed, through a gallows of fifty cubits, on Passover.

Double (punishment) will You bring in an instant upon Utsis (Edom) on Passover.

Let Your hand be strengthened and your right arm uplifted, as on that night when You made holy the festival of Passover.

And you shall say: This is the Passover sacrifice.

אַדִּיר בִּמְלוּכָה בָּחוּר כַּהֲלָכָה. גְּדוּדָיו יֹאמְרוּ לוֹ לְךָ וּלְךָ. לְךָ
כִּי לְךָ. לְךָ אַף לְךָ. לְךָ יְיָ הַמַּמְלָכָה. כִּי לוֹ נָאֶה כִּי לוֹ יָאֶה:
דָּגוּל בִּמְלוּכָה הָדוּר כַּהֲלָכָה. וָתִיקָיו יֹאמְרוּ לוֹ לְךָ וּלְךָ. לְךָ
כִּי לְךָ. לְךָ אַף לְךָ. לְךָ יְיָ הַמַּמְלָכָה. כִּי לוֹ נָאֶה. כִּי לוֹ יָאֶה:
זַכַּאי בִּמְלוּכָה חָסִין כַּהֲלָכָה. טַפְסְרָיו יֹאמְרוּ לוֹ לְךָ וּלְךָ. לְךָ
כִּי לְךָ. לְךָ אַף לְךָ. לְךָ יְיָ הַמַּמְלָכָה. כִּי לוֹ נָאֶה. כִּי לוֹ יָאֶה:
יָחִיד בִּמְלוּכָה כַּבִּיר כַּהֲלָכָה. לִמּוּדָיו יֹאמְרוּ לוֹ לְךָ וּלְךָ. לְךָ
כִּי לְךָ. לְךָ אַף לְךָ. לְךָ יְיָ הַמַּמְלָכָה. כִּי לוֹ נָאֶה. כִּי לוֹ יָאֶה:
מוֹשֵׁל בִּמְלוּכָה נוֹרָא כַּהֲלָכָה. סְבִיבָיו יֹאמְרוּ לוֹ לְךָ וּלְךָ. לְךָ
כִּי לְךָ. לְךָ אַף לְךָ. לְךָ יְיָ הַמַּמְלָכָה. כִּי לוֹ נָאֶה. כִּי לוֹ יָאֶה:
עָנָיו בִּמְלוּכָה פּוֹדֶה כַּהֲלָכָה. צַבָאָיו יֹאמְרוּ לוֹ לְךָ וּלְךָ. לְךָ
כִּי לְךָ. לְךָ אַף לְךָ. לְךָ יְיָ הַמַּמְלָכָה. כִּי לוֹ נָאֶה. כִּי לוֹ יָאֶה:
קָדוֹשׁ בִּמְלוּכָה רַחוּם כַּהֲלָכָה. שִׁנְאַנָּיו יֹאמְרוּ לוֹ לְךָ וּלְךָ.
לְךָ כִּי לְךָ. לְךָ אַף לְךָ. לְךָ יְיָ הַמַּמְלָכָה. כִּי לוֹ נָאֶה. כִּי לוֹ
יָאֶה: תַּקִּיף בִּמְלוּכָה תוֹמֵךְ כַּהֲלָכָה. תְּמִימָיו יֹאמְרוּ לוֹ לְךָ
וּלְךָ. לְךָ כִּי לְךָ. לְךָ אַף לְךָ. לְךָ יְיָ הַמַּמְלָכָה. כִּי לוֹ נָאֶה.
כִּי לוֹ יָאֶה:

Mighty in kingship, perfectly distinguished, His companies (of angels) say to Him: To You, and to You; to You, yes to You, to You; only to You; to You, Hashem, is the sovereignty. To Him (praise) is becoming; to Him (praise) is fitting.

Renowned in kingship, perfectly glorious, His faithful say to Him: To You and to You; to You yes to You; to You, only to You; to You, Hashem, is the sovereignty. To Him (praise) is becoming; to Him (praise) is fitting.

Worthy in kingship, perfectly immune, His princes say to Him: To You and to You; to You yes to You; to You, only to You; to You, Hashem, is the sovereignty. To Him (praise) is becoming; to Him (praise) is fitting.

Unique in kingship, perfectly powerful, His learned ones say to Him: To You and to You; to You yes to You; to You, only to You; to You, Hashem, is the sovereignty. To Him (praise) is becoming; to Him (praise) is fitting.

Commanding in kingship, perfectly awesome, His surrounding (angels) say to Him: To You and to You; to You, yes to You; to You, only to You; to You, Hashem, is the sovereignty. To Him (praise) is becoming; to Him (praise) is fitting.

Modest in kingship, perfectly the Redeemer, His legions say to Him: To You and only to You; to You, yes to You; to You, only to You; to You, Hashem is the sovereignty. To Him (praise) is becoming; to Him (praise) is fitting.

Holy in kingship, perfectly merciful, His snow-white angels say to Him: To You and only to You; to You, yes to You; to You, only to You; to You, Hashem, is the sovereignty. To Him (praise) is becoming; to Him (praise) is fitting.

אַדִּיר הוּא יִבְנֶה בֵּיתוֹ בְּקָרוֹב. בִּמְהֵרָה בִּמְהֵרָה בְּיָמֵינוּ
בְּקָרוֹב. אֵל בְּנֵה. אֵל בְּנֵה. בְּנֵה בֵיתְךָ בְּקָרוֹב: בָּחוּר הוּא.
גָּדוֹל הוּא. דָּגוּל הוּא. יִבְנֶה בֵיתוֹ בְּקָרוֹב. בִּמְהֵרָה בִּמְהֵרָה
בְּיָמֵינוּ בְּקָרוֹב: אֵל בְּנֵה אֵל בְּנֵה. בְּנֵה בֵיתְךָ בְּקָרוֹב: הָדוּר
הוּא. וָתִיק הוּא. זַכַּאי הוּא. חָסִיד הוּא. יִבְנֶה בֵיתוֹ בְּקָרוֹב.
בִּמְהֵרָה בִּמְהֵרָה בְּיָמֵינוּ בְּקָרוֹב: אֵל בְּנֵה אֵל בְּנֵה. בְּנֵה
בֵיתְךָ בְּקָרוֹב: טָהוֹר הוּא. יָחִיד הוּא. כַּבִּיר הוּא. לָמוּד
הוּא. מֶלֶךְ הוּא. נוֹרָא הוּא. סַגִּיב הוּא. עִזּוּז הוּא. פּוֹדֶה
הוּא. צַדִּיק הוּא. יִבְנֶה בֵיתוֹ בְּקָרוֹב. בִּמְהֵרָה בִּמְהֵרָה
בְּיָמֵינוּ בְּקָרוֹב: אֵל בְּנֵה אֵל בְּנֵה. בְּנֵה בֵיתְךָ בְּקָרוֹב: קָדוֹשׁ
הוּא. רַחוּם הוּא. שַׁדַּי הוּא. תַּקִּיף הוּא. יִבְנֶה בֵיתוֹ בְּקָרוֹב.
בִּמְהֵרָה בִּמְהֵרָה בְּיָמֵינוּ בְּקָרוֹב: אֵל בְּנֵה אֵל בְּנֵה. בְּנֵה
בֵיתְךָ בְּקָרוֹב:

He is mighty

אדיר הוא

The Zohar Hakadosh, the textbook of our deepest holy teachings, tells that R. Shimon bar Yochai and his son R. Eliezer were standing on the mountain late one night. It was so late that the whole world was dark. It was right before dawn — we know that whenever the world darkens, dawn is breaking. They were standing there, and it was so dark — what a dark period they lived in right after the destruction of the Temple.

Suddenly came one ray of light, one ray of the sun. All in a second the darkness was gone and the light of day had returned. Another ray; now it was still less dark. Then slowly, slowly, God's greatest light, the sun, came to shine for the world. R. Shimon bar Yochai said to his son, "Laizer, my son, do you see? This is the way that redemption will come to this world. The redemption of Israel, the rebuilding of the Holy City and the Holy Temple, will happen this way: one ray of light, then another ray of light, until the world will be filled with joy and light."

He is mighty. May He soon rebuild His House, speedily, yes speedily, in our days, soon. God, rebuild, God, rebuild, rebuild Your House soon!

He is distinguished, He is great, He is renowned. May He soon rebuild His House, speedily, yes speedily, in our days, soon. God, rebuild, God, rebuild, rebuild Your House soon!

He is glorious, He is faithful, He is worthy, He is gracious. May He soon rebuild His House, speedily, yes speedily, in our days, soon. God, rebuild, God, rebuild, rebuild Your House soon!

He is pure, He is unique, He is powerful, He is learned, He is majestic, He is awesome, He is sublime, He is all-powerful, He is the Redeemer, He is righteous. May he soon rebuild His House, speedily, yes speedily, in our days, soon. God, rebuild, God rebuild, rebuild Your House soon!

He is holy, He is merciful, He is Almighty, He is forceful. May He soon rebuild His House, speedily, yes speedily, in our days, soon. God, rebuild, God, rebuild, rebuild Your House soon!

ותיק הוא

He is faithful

"*Vasik hu*, He is faithful." According to our tradition, the Holy Temple in Jerusalem was destroyed because we didn't love each other enough. Every-

אֶחָד מִי יוֹדֵעַ. אֶחָד אֲנִי יוֹדֵעַ. אֶחָד אֱלֹהֵינוּ שֶׁבַּשָּׁמַיִם
וּבָאָרֶץ:

שְׁנַיִם מִי יוֹדֵעַ. שְׁנַיִם אֲנִי יוֹדֵעַ. שְׁנֵי לוּחוֹת הַבְּרִית. אֶחָד
אֱלֹהֵינוּ שֶׁבַּשָּׁמַיִם וּבָאָרֶץ:

body's Holy Temple, marriage, gets broken for the same reason: because we
don't love each other enough. There's a Holy Temple between parents and
children, between friends, nations; but it gets destroyed because we don't
love each other. Everybody knows that Yirmiyahu Hanavi wrote the Book of
Lamentations. All the holy rabbis agree that he wrote it before the Destruction, when he saw how pathetic we were. He wrote it then, because after the
Destruction there's nothing to write any more. We see it all.

The last passage in Lamentations says, "lamah lanetzach tishkacheinu,
why do You forget us forever? Hashiveinu eilecha v'nashuvah, bring us back
to You and we'll come back." I want to share something deep with you.
Imagine that a husband and a wife have a fight, God forbid, and get divorced. Them they meet two thousand years later, and they're still angry at
each other. That means they still love each other, because you're not angry
at someone you don't love. We say to the One, to the Only One, "You're still
angry at us after two thousand years — gevalt, how You must love us! Please
take us back. Master of the world, hold out Your hand. We're holding out
our hand."

אחד מי יודע   Who knows one?

In Hebrew, pashut means "simple." It doesn't mean stupid, it means that
something isn't complicated, that it's made up of one piece. Most of us are
made up of a hundred people all mixed together in one place, but there's
always something inside each of us that isn't split. It's whole, complete. We
need to reach that part inside of us which is one piece, one entity. It's the
most God-like part of us. God is One; He's not a hundred, He's One. If we're
serving God with this one piece, we can mamash be totally connected to
Him.

> Who knows one? I know one: One is our God, in heaven and on earth.
>
> Who knows two? I know two: two are the Tablets of the Covenant; One is our God, in heaven and on earth.

שני לוחות הברית   Two Tablets of the Covenant

The mind is capable of understanding the deepest depths. The heart is capable of having something carved in it like stone. The Torah says that the two tablets were like a heart, and the Ten Commandments were carved into them, not written on them. Suppose someone says, "Why do you need to hear the Ten Commandments on *Har Sinai?* Before God told us not to kill, didn't we know not to kill, not to steal? Anyone decent knows not to steal." You know what God did for us on *Har Sinai?* He didn't just tell us like an article in the newspaper, He carved the Torah into us. The holy Izhbitzer Rebbe says, "How did God carve into us not to kill? Did He carve into us the words 'don't kill'? If you're already on such a low level that you want to kill, you don't stop because it's forbidden." He answered, "God opened gates for us, and then we knew how precious life is. If you have any taste of how precious each and every life is, you can't kill."

When God said "Don't steal," He opened gates for us, and the realization was so deep for us, the relationship between everything I have and myself. It's not just a law that this thing here belongs to me and you shouldn't steal it. Sometimes when you steal something from somebody you take away his soul. You can kill him — his soul was so attached to this thing, he could die without it.

When God said "Honor your father and mother," He showed us how special it is to bring children down to this world. Children realize, "My father and mother *mamash* brought me into this world."

If you keep every Shabbos to the letter of the law but it isn't carved into your heart, you haven't kept Shabbos. It has to be carved in until you realize, "I can never do without it"; until it reaches the deepest, highest place in your heart. This is keeping Shabbos.

שְׁלשָׁה מִי יוֹדֵעַ. שְׁלשָׁה אֲנִי יוֹדֵעַ. שְׁלשָׁה אָבוֹת. שְׁנֵי
לוּחוֹת הַבְּרִית. אֶחָד אֱלֹהֵינוּ שֶׁבַּשָּׁמַיִם וּבָאָרֶץ:
אַרְבַּע מִי יוֹדֵעַ. אַרְבַּע אֲנִי יוֹדֵעַ. אַרְבַּע אִמָּהוֹת. שְׁלשָׁה
אָבוֹת. שְׁנֵי לוּחוֹת הַבְּרִית. אֶחָד אֱלֹהֵינוּ שֶׁבַּשָּׁמַיִם וּבָאָרֶץ:
חֲמִשָּׁה מִי יוֹדֵעַ. חֲמִשָּׁה אֲנִי יוֹדֵעַ. חֲמִשָּׁה חוּמְשֵׁי תוֹרָה.
אַרְבַּע אִמָּהוֹת. שְׁלשָׁה אָבוֹת. שְׁנֵי לוּחוֹת הַבְּרִית. אֶחָד
אֱלֹהֵינוּ שֶׁבַּשָּׁמַיִם וּבָאָרֶץ:
שִׁשָּׁה מִי יוֹדֵעַ. שִׁשָּׁה אֲנִי יוֹדֵעַ. שִׁשָּׁה סִדְרֵי מִשְׁנָה.
חֲמִשָּׁה חוּמְשֵׁי תוֹרָה. אַרְבַּע אִמָּהוֹת. שְׁלשָׁה אָבוֹת. שְׁנֵי
לוּחוֹת הַבְּרִית. אֶחָד אֱלֹהֵינוּ שֶׁבַּשָּׁמַיִם וּבָאָרֶץ:
שִׁבְעָה מִי יוֹדֵעַ. שִׁבְעָה אֲנִי יוֹדֵעַ. שִׁבְעָה יְמֵי שַׁבַּתָּא.
שִׁשָּׁה סִדְרֵי מִשְׁנָה. חֲמִשָּׁה חוּמְשֵׁי תוֹרָה. אַרְבַּע אִמָּהוֹת.
שְׁלשָׁה אָבוֹת. שְׁנֵי לוּחוֹת הַבְּרִית. אֶחָד אֱלֹהֵינוּ
שֶׁבַּשָּׁמַיִם וּבָאָרֶץ:
שְׁמוֹנָה מִי יוֹדֵעַ. שְׁמוֹנָה אֲנִי יוֹדֵעַ. שְׁמוֹנָה יְמֵי מִילָה.
שִׁבְעָה יְמֵי שַׁבַּתָּא. שִׁשָּׁה סִדְרֵי מִשְׁנָה. חֲמִשָּׁה חוּמְשֵׁי
תוֹרָה. אַרְבַּע אִמָּהוֹת. שְׁלשָׁה אָבוֹת. שְׁנֵי לוּחוֹת הַבְּרִית.
אֶחָד אֱלֹהֵינוּ שֶׁבַּשָּׁמַיִם וּבָאָרֶץ:

Who knows three? I know three: three are the Patriarchs; two are the Tablets of the Covenant; One is our God, in heaven and on earth.

Who knows four? I know four: four are the Matriarchs; three are the Patriarchs; two are the Tablets of the Covenant; One is our God, in heaven and on earth.

Who knows five? I know five: five are the Books of the Torah; four are the Matriarchs; three are the Patriarchs; two are the Tablets of the Covenant; One is our God, in heaven and on earth.

Who knows six? I know six: six are the Orders of the Mishnah; five are the Books of the Torah; four are the Matriarchs; three are the Patriarchs; two are the Tablets of the Covenant; One is our God, in heaven and on earth.

Who know seven? I know seven: seven are the days of the week; six are the Orders of the Mishnah; five are the Books of the Torah; four are the Matriarchs; three are the Patriarchs; two are the Tablets of the Covenant; One is our God, in heaven and on earth.

Who knows eight? I know eight: eight are the days to circumcision; seven are the days of the week; six are the Orders of the Mishnah; five are the Books of the Torah; four are the Matriarchs; three are the Patriarchs; two are the Tablets of the Covenant; One is our God, in heaven and on earth.

תִּשְׁעָה מִי יוֹדֵעַ. תִּשְׁעָה אֲנִי יוֹדֵעַ. תִּשְׁעָה יַרְחֵי לֵידָה.
שְׁמוֹנָה יְמֵי מִילָה. שִׁבְעָה יְמֵי שַׁבַּתָּא. שִׁשָּׁה סִדְרֵי
מִשְׁנָה. חֲמִשָּׁה חוּמְשֵׁי תוֹרָה. אַרְבַּע אִמָּהוֹת. שְׁלֹשָׁה
אָבוֹת. שְׁנֵי לוּחוֹת הַבְּרִית. אֶחָד אֱלֹהֵינוּ שֶׁבַּשָּׁמַיִם וּבָאָרֶץ:
עֲשָׂרָה מִי יוֹדֵעַ. עֲשָׂרָה אֲנִי יוֹדֵעַ. עֲשָׂרָה דִבְּרַיָּא. תִּשְׁעָה
יַרְחֵי לֵידָה. שְׁמוֹנָה יְמֵי מִילָה. שִׁבְעָה יְמֵי שַׁבַּתָּא. שִׁשָּׁה
סִדְרֵי מִשְׁנָה. חֲמִשָּׁה חוּמְשֵׁי תוֹרָה. אַרְבַּע אִמָּהוֹת.
שְׁלֹשָׁה אָבוֹת. שְׁנֵי לוּחוֹת הַבְּרִית. אֶחָד אֱלֹהֵינוּ
שֶׁבַּשָּׁמַיִם וּבָאָרֶץ:

אַחַד עָשָׂר מִי יוֹדֵעַ. אַחַד עָשָׂר אֲנִי יוֹדֵעַ. אַחַד עָשָׂר
כּוֹכְבַיָּא. עֲשָׂרָה דִבְּרַיָּא. תִּשְׁעָה יַרְחֵי לֵידָה. שְׁמוֹנָה יְמֵי
מִילָה. שִׁבְעָה יְמֵי שַׁבַּתָּא. שִׁשָּׁה סִדְרֵי מִשְׁנָה. חֲמִשָּׁה
חוּמְשֵׁי תוֹרָה. אַרְבַּע אִמָּהוֹת. שְׁלֹשָׁה אָבוֹת. שְׁנֵי לוּחוֹת
הַבְּרִית. אֶחָד אֱלֹהֵינוּ שֶׁבַּשָּׁמַיִם וּבָאָרֶץ:

Who knows nine? I know nine: nine are the months of pregnancy; eight are the days to circumcision; seven are the days of the week; six are the Orders of the Mishnah; five are the Books of the Torah; four are the Matriarchs; three are the Patriarchs; two are the Tablets of the Covenant; One is our God, in heaven and on earth.

Who knows ten? I know ten: ten are the Ten Commandments; nine are the months of pregnancy; eight are the days to circumcision; seven are the days of the week; six are the Orders of the Mishnah; five are the Books of the Torah; four are the Matriarchs; three are the Patriarchs; two are the Tablets of the Covenant; One is our God, in heaven and on earth.

Who knows eleven? I know eleven: eleven are the stars (in Yosef's dream); ten are the Ten Commandments; nine are the months of pregnancy; eight are the days to circumcision; seven are the days of the week; six are the Orders of the Mishnah; five are the Books of the Torah; four are the Matriarchs; three are the Patriarchs; two are the Tablets of the Covenant; One is our God, in heaven and on earth.

שְׁנֵים עָשָׂר מִי יוֹדֵעַ. שְׁנֵים עָשָׂר אֲנִי יוֹדֵעַ. שְׁנֵים עָשָׂר
שִׁבְטַיָּא. אַחַד עָשָׂר כּוֹכְבַיָּא. עֲשָׂרָה דִבְּרַיָּא. תִּשְׁעָה יַרְחֵי
לֵידָה. שְׁמוֹנָה יְמֵי מִילָה. שִׁבְעָה יְמֵי שַׁבַּתָּא. שִׁשָּׁה סִדְרֵי
מִשְׁנָה. חֲמִשָּׁה חוּמְשֵׁי תוֹרָה. אַרְבַּע אִמָּהוֹת. שְׁלֹשָׁה
אָבוֹת. שְׁנֵי לוּחוֹת הַבְּרִית. אֶחָד אֱלֹהֵינוּ שֶׁבַּשָּׁמַיִם וּבָאָרֶץ:

שְׁלֹשָׁה עָשָׂר מִי יוֹדֵעַ. שְׁלֹשָׁה עָשָׂר אֲנִי יוֹדֵעַ. שְׁלֹשָׁה
עָשָׂר מִדַּיָּא. שְׁנֵים עָשָׂר שִׁבְטַיָּא. אַחַד עָשָׂר כּוֹכְבַיָּא.
עֲשָׂרָה דִבְּרַיָּא. תִּשְׁעָה יַרְחֵי לֵידָה. שְׁמוֹנָה יְמֵי מִילָה.
שִׁבְעָה יְמֵי שַׁבַּתָּא. שִׁשָּׁה סִדְרֵי מִשְׁנָה. חֲמִשָּׁה חוּמְשֵׁי
תוֹרָה. אַרְבַּע אִמָּהוֹת. שְׁלֹשָׁה אָבוֹת. שְׁנֵי לוּחוֹת הַבְּרִית.
אֶחָד אֱלֹהֵינוּ שֶׁבַּשָּׁמַיִם וּבָאָרֶץ:

Who knows twelve? I know twelve: twelve are the tribes (of Israel); eleven are the stars (in Yosef's dream); ten are the Ten Commandments; nine are the months of pregnancy; eight are the days to circumcision; seven are the days of the week; six are the Orders of the Mishnah; five are the Books of the Torah; four are the Matriarchs; three are the Patriarchs; two are the Tablets of the Covenant; One is our God, in heaven and on earth.

Who knows thirteen? In know thirteen: thirteen are the attributes of God; twelve are the tribes (of Israel); eleven are the stars (in Yosef's dream); ten are the Ten Commandments; nine are the months of pregnancy; eight are the days to circumcision; seven are the days of the week; six are the Orders of the Mishnah; five are the Books of the Torah; four are the Matriarchs; three are the Patriarchs; two are the Tablets of the Covenant; One is our God, in heaven and on earth.

חַד גַּדְיָא. חַד גַּדְיָא. דְּזַבִּין אַבָּא בִּתְרֵי זוּזֵי.
חַד גַּדְיָא. חַד גַּדְיָא:
וְאָתָא שׁוּנְרָא. וְאָכְלָה לְגַדְיָא. דְּזַבִּין אַבָּא בִּתְרֵי זוּזֵי. חַד
גַּדְיָא. חַד גַּדְיָא:
וְאָתָא כַלְבָּא. וְנָשַׁךְ לְשׁוּנְרָא. דְּאָכְלָה לְגַדְיָא. דְּזַבִּין אַבָּא
בִּתְרֵי זוּזֵי. חַד גַּדְיָא חַד גַּדְיָא:
וְאָתָא חוּטְרָא. וְהִכָּה לְכַלְבָּא. דְּנָשַׁךְ לְשׁוּנְרָא. דְּאָכְלָה
לְגַדְיָא. דְּזַבִּין אַבָּא בִּתְרֵי זוּזֵי. חַד גַּדְיָא. חַד גַּדְיָא:
וְאָתָא נוּרָא. וְשָׂרַף לְחוּטְרָא. דְּהִכָּה לְכַלְבָּא. דְּנָשַׁךְ
לְשׁוּנְרָא. דְּאָכְלָה לְגַדְיָא. דְּזַבִּין אַבָּא בִּתְרֵי זוּזֵי. חַד גַּדְיָא.
חַד גַּדְיָא:
וְאָתָא מַיָּא. וְכָבָה לְנוּרָא. דְּשָׂרַף לְחוּטְרָא. דְּהִכָּה לְכַלְבָּא.
דְּנָשַׁךְ לְשׁוּנְרָא. דְּאָכְלָה לְגַדְיָא. דְּזַבִּין אַבָּא בִּתְרֵי זוּזֵי.
חַד גַּדְיָא. חַד גַּדְיָא:
וְאָתָא תוֹרָא. וְשָׁתָה לְמַיָּא. דְּכָבָה לְנוּרָא. דְּשָׂרַף לְחוּטְרָא.
דְּהִכָּה לְכַלְבָּא. דְּנָשַׁךְ לְשׁוּנְרָא. דְּאָכְלָה לְגַדְיָא. דְּזַבִּין
אַבָּא בִּתְרֵי זוּזֵי. חַד גַּדְיָא. חַד גַּדְיָא:

One little goat, one little goat, that father bought for two zuzim, one little goat, one little goat.

And then came a cat and ate the goat that father bought for two zuzim, one little goat, one little goat.

And then came a dog and bit the cat, that ate the goat that father bought for two zuzim, one little goat, one little goat.

And then came a stick and beat the dog, that bit the cat, that ate the goat that father bought for two zuzim, one little goat, one little goat.

And then came a fire and burnt the stick, that beat the dog, that bit the cat, that ate the goat that father bought for two zuzim, one little goat, one little goat.

And then came water and put out the fire, that burnt the stick, that beat the dog, that bit the cat, that ate the goat that father bought for two zuzim, one little goat, one little goat.

And then came an ox and drank the water, that put out the fire, that burnt the stick, that beat the dog, that bit the cat, that ate the goat, that father bought for two zuzim, one little goat, one little goat.

וְאָתָא הַשׁוֹחֵט. וְשָׁחַט לְתוֹרָא. דְּשָׁתָה לְמַיָּא. דְּכָבָה
לְנוּרָא. דְּשָׂרַף לְחוּטְרָא. דְּהִכָּה לְכַלְבָּא. דְּנָשַׁךְ לְשׁוּנְרָא.
דְּאָכְלָה לְגַדְיָא. דְּזַבִּין אַבָּא בִּתְרֵי זוּזֵי. חַד גַּדְיָא. חַד
גַּדְיָא:

וְאָתָא מַלְאַךְ הַמָּוֶת. וְשָׁחַט לְשׁוֹחֵט. דְּשָׁחַט לְתוֹרָא.
דְּשָׁתָה לְמַיָּא. דְּכָבָה לְנוּרָא. דְּשָׂרַף לְחוּטְרָא. דְּהִכָּה
לְכַלְבָּא. דְּנָשַׁךְ לְשׁוּנְרָא. דְּאָכְלָא לְגַדְיָא. דְּזַבִּין אַבָּא
בִּתְרֵי זוּזֵי. חַד גַּדְיָא. חַד גַּדְיָא:

וְאָתָא הַקָּדוֹשׁ בָּרוּךְ הוּא. וְשָׁחַט לְמַלְאַךְ הַמָּוֶת. דְּשָׁחַט
לְשׁוֹחֵט. דְּשָׁחַט לְתוֹרָא. דְּשָׁתָה לְמַיָּא. דְּכָבָה לְנוּרָא.
דְּשָׂרַף לְחוּטְרָא. דְּהִכָּה לְכַלְבָּא. דְּנָשַׁךְ לְשׁוּנְרָא. דְּאָכְלָא
לְגַדְיָא. דְּזַבִּין אַבָּא בִּתְרֵי זוּזֵי. חַד גַּדְיָא. חַד גַּדְיָא:

A slaughterer then came and slaughtered the ox, that drank the water, that put out the fire, that burnt the stick, that beat the dog, that bit the cat, that ate the goat, that father bought for two zuzim, one little goat, one little goat.

And then came the angel of death and slew the slaughterer, who slaughtered the ox, that drank the water, that put out the fire, that burnt the stick, that beat the dog, that bit the cat, that ate the goat, that father bought for two zuzim, one little goat, one little goat.

And then came The Holy One, blessed is He, and killed the angel of death, who slew the slaughterer, who slaughtered the ox, that drank the water, that put out the fire, that burnt the stick, that beat the dog, that bit the cat, that ate the goat that father bought for two zuzim, one little goat, one little goat.

For those making Second Seder: whoever did not count the Omer after Maariv on the second night of Pesach should count now.

ספירת העומר

הִנְנִי מוּכָן וּמְזֻמָּן לְקַיֵּם מִצְוַת עֲשֵׂה שֶׁל סְפִירַת הָעֹמֶר כְּמוֹ שֶׁכָּתוּב בַּתּוֹרָה: וּסְפַרְתֶּם לָכֶם מִמָּחֳרַת הַשַּׁבָּת מִיּוֹם הֲבִיאֲכֶם אֶת עֹמֶר הַתְּנוּפָה שֶׁבַע שַׁבָּתוֹת תְּמִימֹת תִּהְיֶינָה: עַד מִמָּחֳרַת הַשַּׁבָּת הַשְּׁבִיעִת תִּסְפְּרוּ חֲמִשִּׁים יוֹם וְהִקְרַבְתֶּם מִנְחָה חֲדָשָׁה לַיְיָ: וִיהִי נֹעַם יְיָ אֱלֹהֵינוּ עָלֵינוּ וּמַעֲשֵׂה יָדֵינוּ כּוֹנְנָה עָלֵינוּ וּמַעֲשֵׂה יָדֵינוּ כּוֹנְנֵהוּ:

בָּרוּךְ אַתָּה יְיָ אֱלֹהֵינוּ מֶלֶךְ הָעוֹלָם, אֲשֶׁר קִדְּשָׁנוּ בְּמִצְוֹתָיו וְצִוָּנוּ עַל סְפִירַת הָעֹמֶר.

טז בניסן, א' של חול המועד

הַיּוֹם יוֹם אֶחָד לָעֹמֶר. חסד שבחסד

יז בניסן, ב' של חול המועד

הַיּוֹם שְׁנֵי יָמִים לָעֹמֶר. גבורה שבחסד

הָרַחֲמָן הוּא יַחֲזִיר לָנוּ עֲבוֹדַת בֵּית הַמִּקְדָּשׁ לִמְקוֹמָהּ, בִּמְהֵרָה בְיָמֵינוּ אָמֵן סֶלָה.

ספירת העומר   **Counting the Omer**

When someone puts on *tefillin* or shakes his *lulav*, he doesn't say, "Master of the world, I'm ready for the Holy Temple." I'm sure it's important, but we don't say it. There is only one mitzvah in the world that after doing it we say, "Master of the world, take me back to the Holy Temple." That's when we count the Omer.

Counting the Omer

For those making Second Seder: whoever did not count the Omer after Maariv on the second night of Pesach should count now.

Blessed are You, Hashem, our God, King of the universe, Who has sanctified us with His commandments and commanded us to count the Omer.

Today is the first day of Omer.

May it be Your will, Hashem, our God and God of our fathers, that the Holy Temple be rebuilt, speedily in our days, and give us our portion in Your Torah. And there we will serve You with awe as in days of old and as in former years.

You know what it is to be in exile? You know what real *galus* is? For me, it's that one day is like another, one minute is like another — just pushing my days through, pushing my nights through. I'm not doing anything wrong, but life isn't exciting; life is boring.

I want you really to open your hearts in the deepest way. One of our holiest masters, about a hundred and fifty years ago, was the holy Or Hameir, "the shining light." He was one of the greatest pupils of the Seer of Lublin. One night he stopped at an inn, a *kretchmere*. And you know, when a holy rabbi comes in the innkeeper says, "I have a special room for you." This innkeeper gave the Or Hameir a beautiful room which had a big clock hanging on the wall.

All night long the Or Hameir couldn't sleep; he walked up and down. You know, in a little wooden house, like those *kretchmeres*, when you walk to the right the whole house bends right, and when you walk left the whole house bends left. So the poor innkeeper couldn't sleep either. Finally, at three o'clock in the morning, the innkeeper decided it was no use trying any longer. "Let's make some hot tea," he thought, "and bring it to the holy rabbi." The innkeeper knocked on the door and brought in the tea. Then he asked, "Holy rabbi, don't you like the bed, or is it something else? Why don't you sleep?"

"Oy no," answered the holy Or Hameir, "God forbid! This is a beautiful room." The innkeeper asked, "So why can't you sleep?" The Rebbe answered, "Let me ask you something. This big clock hanging on the wall, did it by any chance belong to my holy master, the Seer of Lublin?" The innkeeper replied, "Yes, but don't think I stole it. His son was here for two weeks and he couldn't pay. So he pawned this clock and he'll come back in a few weeks to redeem it. But," he said, "I don't understand. What does your sleeping have to do with the clock?"

The holy Or Hameir replied, "My dear friend, let me tell you something. There are two kinds of clocks in the world. Let's say a clock strikes one, two, three, or four. All the ordinary clocks in the world say 'One hour has passed, one more hour has passed, there's one hour less, another hour less.' *Oy vey,* when you hear that, you think, 'Who needs the whole thing? Let's go to sleep and forget it all.' But then there is the Seer of Lublin's clock. It says, 'One hour closer to Mashiach, another hour closer to the great day.' One hour closer to redemption, one hour closer to everything holy and beautiful — you get so excited, how can you sleep?"

So you see, I want to bless you and me and all of us. We need a completely different clock, a real time change. May we have the power of extracting ourselves from time; but above all, my blessing is that every hour you may realize we're getting closer.

I was once walking on the beach in Tel Aviv, and I saw a young man sitting there and crying. I walked up to him and said, "Why are you crying, my friend?" He says, "You know something? I have everything: I have money, I have pleasures — but I also have a soul, and I don't know what to do with it."

Do you know, my beautiful friends, there were moments, days, when we could have fixed the world and we could have fixed our own lives. But we were in exile, and we didn't even see the opportunity. When we count the Omer we say, "Master of the world, I'm counting again, I'm a free person again. I know what precious moments are all about. When the moment of redemption comes, I'm ready." Between people, too — do you know how many husbands and wives could have made it if they had watched for the moments when they could fix their lives and be close again?

Between us and the world, too — the sad truth is that there were great moments when Israel and the world could have made peace. But we didn't watch for the moments. We didn't count the day.

You know what R. Shimon bar Yochai says? The first sign of a holy person is that he's full of joy, full of life. You know what holy means? That whatever you do, you do it with all your heart and all your might. What does it mean that Hashem is holy? That He's always there. Holy means that I'm always there when someone needs me.

You know what a good friend is? You call him up and ask, "Can you please do me a favor?" and he says, "Can you call me back in ten minutes? Right now I'm very busy." You know what a holy friend is? You need a favor, and it's done already; you didn't even have to ask. You and I — we need holy friends, holy moments.

I'm sure it's clear to you and me — let's imagine for a moment what would be if all the Jews in the world were the way Hashem wants us to be. The world would be ours. If all of us were shining with holiness and sweetness, if all of us shone with God's oneness, any human being that saw us on the street would run after us and say, "Hey! You know, there's something that I want to know so badly. Can you tell it to me?" What a world! "*U've-khein tein kavod, Hashem, l'amecha*, give honor to Your people, *v'sikvah tovah*, good hope to the ones who seek You, *simchah v'sason*, happiness and rejoicing and the coming of the Mashiach."

Peace in Yerushalayim. Peace in Your holy city. Peace in every land. Peace in every city. Peace in every street. Let there be peace. Just one more tear, just one more prayer, just one more song, just one more day, just one more sunset, just one more night. Just for my children, just for your children, just for all of God's children, let there be peace.

We count the Omer and we say, "*Harachaman*, may the Merciful One bring back the Temple service to us." May the Holy One take us back, bring us back, bring us close again to the Holy Temple to serve You — the One, the Only One.

The *heilige* Rebbe Nachman of Breslav considered himself a personal pupil of R. Shimon bar Yochai. Rebbe Nachman, the holy master, says, "In order to serve God you have to learn, you have to know, three lessons. The first lesson is that you must learn how to walk, and you must learn how to stand. When you do a mitzvah, when you do something good, you're walking in God's ways. When you're praying, you stand before the Only One. But only those who are walking know how to stand, and only those who are standing know how to walk. This is the first lesson.

"The second lesson is a bit harder: learn how to fall and how to get up. If you are falling, don't be sad: you know God is teaching you how to get up. If you don't fall, how can the One, the Only One, teach you how to get up?

So when you're falling, let your heart be filled with joy, because the Only One, who knows and can teach you, is showing you how to get up."

The third lesson is the hardest: I have a feeling that this lesson is about you and me, about all of us. What do you do when you're falling and can't get up? What do you do when your heart is so broken, your spirit is so destroyed, that there's nothing to hope for, nothing to look back to? Rebbe Nachman says, "In the meantime, keep on walking; in the meantime, keep on standing; in the meantime, keep on singing; in the meantime, keep on praying; in the meantime, keep on loving, until the day when it's revealed to you that you never fell. How could it be possible to fall when the Only One is holding you so close?"

Glossary

amar Abayei	"Abaye" (an Amora) "says"
Baal Shem Tov	founder of the Chassidic movement. He was born in the year 5458 and died on the sixth of Sivan 5520.
Bar Cochba	Shimon ben Kosiba was renamed Bar Cochba ("son of a star"), when, in the year 117 BCE, he led an uprising against the Romans. Rabbi Akiva was his staunch supporter and proclaimed him to be worthy of being the Mashiach. He was briefly successful in establishing his kingship over the Jewish Nation.
Bavli	the Babylonian Talmud
Beis Hamikdash	the Holy Temple
Belz	a city in Hungary, home of the Belzer Chassidic Dynasty
bobbe	grandmother (Yiddish)
Bobover	the Bobover Rebbe, R. Shlomo Halberstam, who resided in New York until his recent passing
challah	specially baked loaves of bread for the Sabbath meals
chas veshalom	God forbid
Chassidim	followers of a Chassidic Rabbi
chuppah	wedding canopy
davening	praying
Gan Eden	Garden of Eden, also, figuratively the reward of the World to Come
Gemara	Talmud
gevalt	a Yiddish exclamation, meaning more or less, "tremendous!"
goy	gentile
heilige	holy (Yiddish)
hesped	eulogy
Izhbitzer	R. Mordechai Yosef of Izhbitz, author of *Mei Hashiloach,* died 5614
Kaliscer	R. Avraham of Kalisc, made *aliyah* to the Holy Land along with R. Mendele Vitebsker. He died on the fourth of Shevat 5570.
Karliner	R. Aaron Hagadol ("the great") of Karlin, founder of the Karlin dynasty, a disciple of the Mezritcher Maggid and leader of the Chassidim in Lithuania. Born 5496, died 5532.

kittel	a white robe traditionally worn by a bridegroom, also worn by many on Seder night and the High Holy Days (Yiddish)
kleiner siddur	small prayer book
Kotzker	R. Menachem of Kotzk, a disciple of R. Simchah Bunim of Priskha, a great student of the Baal Shem Tov. Renowned for his unique sharpness. Born 5547, died 5619.
Koznitzer Maggid	a disciple of R. Elimelech, one of the founders of the Chassidic movement in Poland, a genius in Torah, author of *Avodas Yisrael*. Born 5496, died 5575.
lamdan	a competent scholar
l'chaim	"to life," the traditional Jewish toast
licht	candle, lamp (Yiddish)
mamash	actually, really
Mashiach	the Messiah
masechta	tractate (of the Talmud)
mikvah	ritual bath
mitzvah	a commandment; also applied to Rabbinic ordinances
Motzaei Shabbos	Saturday Night
navi	prophet
nebach	sad to say (Yiddish)
neshama	soul
niggun	tune
Odessa	a city in Russia
Or Hameir	R. Zev Volf, the Rabbi of Zhitomir. A talmid of the Maggid. He wrote *Or Hameir* and was called after his book. Died 5560.
peyos	sidelocks
pikuach nefesh	danger to life
Pshischa	a town in the Ukraine where R. Simcha Bunim was the Chassidic Rebbe.
Rashi	eleventh-century scholar whose commentaries on the Torah and Talmud are in standard use until this day.
rachmanus	mercy; also, figuratively, "what a pity"
Radziminer	a student of R. Simchah Bunim of Pshischa. Born 5552, died 5634.
R. Achai Gaon	one of the Gaonim, the great sages who lived after the completion of the Talmud
R. Akiva Eiger	a renowed sage who wrote on the Mishnah, Talmud and Shulchan Aruch. Died 5598.
R. Asher Karliner	son and student of R. Aaron Hagadol of Karlin. Born 5496, died 5532.

R. Dovid Lelover   founder of Lelov's Chassidic dynasty, a student of R. Elimelech of Lizhensk. Born 5506, died 5574.

Rebbe Elimelech   a student of the Mezritcher Maggid, Rebbe of Lizhensk, one of the great men of the Chassidic movement. His work, *Noam Elimelech* (by whose name he himself is called), is one of the basic books of Chassidus. Died 5546.

R. Mendel   a student of the *Noam Elimelech*, Rebbe of Riminov and author of several Chassidic works. There were dozens of Chassidic Rebbes who considered themselves students of R. Mendel. Died 5575.

R. Mendel Vitebsker
          made *aliyah* to the Holy Land with three hundred followers and settled in Safed. He then moved to Tiberias, where he died and was buried in the year 5548.

R. Nachman   of Bratzlav (*also* Breslav), a grandson of the Baal Shem Tov. Born on Rosh Chodesh Nissan 5532, died 5571.

R. Nachum Tchernobiler
          founder of the Tchernobil Chassidic dynasty, a student of the Baal Shem Tov. He wrote *Meor Einayim*. Born 5490, died 5558.

R. Shimon bar Yochai
          a Tanna, author of the Zohar

R. Tzvi Elimelech   of Dinov, founder of Dinov's Chassidic dynasty. Born 5543, died 5601.

R. Yisrael Viletnik   a student of R. Mordechai of Tchernobil. He was very close to R. Levi Yitzchak of Berditchev, and was widely renowned for his wisdom. His gravesite is considered holy even by the gentiles up until today. Born 5549. Died 5610.

R. Yisroel Vizhnitz   author of *Ahavas Yisrael*. Born 5620, died 5696.

Rebbe   teacher; also, spiritual leader of a group of people

Rozhiner   R. Yisrael of Rozhin, a great-grandson of the Mezritcher Maggid, founder of Rozhin's Chassidic dynasty. Born 5567, died 5611.

Rosh Hashanah   the Jewish New Year

Spoler Zaide   a student of the Baal Shem Tov and R. Pinchas of Koritz, Rebbe of Spole (pronounced shpo-leh), Born 5485, died 5572.

Seer of Lublin   a student of the Mezritcher Maggid and of R. Elimelech of Lizhensk. Many great Rebbes of Poland were his students. Born 5505, died Tisha B'av 5575.

sefarim	books
Shalom Aleichem	"Greetings, ministering angels": the welcome song customarily sung to greet the angels on Shabbos night.
Shema	"Hear, O Israel": declaration recited twice a day and on one's death bed
Sheva Berachos	the seven blessings recited over a newlywed couple; also, figuratively, the seven days of rejoicing after a wedding
shidduch	traditional meeting between two young people arranged by a matchmaker
shul	synagogue
siyata dishmaya	divine aid
Talmud Bavli	Babylonian Talmud
Tanna d'vei Eliyahu	a Midrash written by R. Anan related what he learned from Elijah the Prophet
Tatte zisse	sweet father (Yiddish)
teshuvah	repentance
Tosafos	commentary printed along with the Talmud
tzitzis	fringes worn on the corners of a four-cornered garment in order to remind one of his obligations to God
Vizhnitzer	R. Menachem of Vizhnitz, author of *Tzemach Tzadik*. Born 5590, died 5645.
yarmulke	skullcap (Yiddish)
Yerushalmi	the Jerusalem Talmud
Yerushalayim	Jerusalem
yeshivah	school of Jewish learning
Yeshuas Yaakov	R. Yaakov Orenstein, known as one of the foremost scholars of his generation; served as head of the Rabbinic Court in Levov. Died 21 Av 5599.
Yid	Jew
Yidden	Jews
Yiddishkeit	the Jewish way of living
Yom Kippur	Day of Atonement
Yirmiyahu Hanavi	the Prophet Jeremiah
Zaide	Grandfather (Yiddish)
Zohar Hakadosh	the Holy Zohar, a Kabbalistic work authored by Rabbi Shimon Bar Yochai.